Margam Castle

John Vivian Hughes

West Glamorgan Archive Service

1998

First published 1981

Published by the West Glamorgan Archive Service

Margam Castle from the south east. A rare daguerrotype taken on March 9, 1841 by the Reverend Calvert Jones of Swansea, a great friend of C. R. M. Talbot.
(National Library of Wales)

RHAGAIR

Gyda phleser mawr yr ysgrifennaf y rhagair yma i ail-gyhoeddiad y traethawd ar Gastell Margam gan Mr John Vivian Hughes.

Rydym ar drothwy Mileniwm newydd mewn oes dechnolegol, ond mae nodweddion arbennig Margam yn dal i'n swyno - y teimlad o ehangder, yr ymwybyddiaeth ei fod yn fangre hanesyddol, yr amgylchedd sy'n rhoi hwb i'r galon.

Ni all unrhyw Gyngor Lleol ond bod yn ofalwr o dreftadaeth Margam, a thrwy waith gwerthfawr cyn awdurdod Gorllewin Morgannwg, cafodd castell Margam ei adfer a'i gadw'n ddiogel. Gobaith cyngor newydd Bwrdeistref Sirol Castell Nedd Port Talbot yw dal ymlaen â'r gwaith.

Ymhlith yr amcanion diweddaraf mae cynllun sefydlu Canolfan Astudiaethau'r Amgylchedd i oedolion a phobl ifanc ym Margam, mewn partneriaeth â'r Cyngor Astudiaethau Maes, yn ogystal a chynllun i adfer rhai o erddi Margam i'w cyflwr gwreiddiol. Bydd angen darganfod gwahanol ffyrdd i ariannu'r amcanion yma, ond mae'r Awdurdod newydd yn barod i fwrw mlaen.

Mae'r ffaith bod Pwyllgor Archifau Gorllewin Morgannwg wedi cytuno i ail-gyhoeddi'r portread bychan pwysig yma o hanes lleol yn peri pleser mawr imi.

Ken Sawyers
Prif Swyddog
Cyngor Bwrdeistref Sirol Castell-Nedd Port Talbot
1998

FOREWORD

It gives me great pleasure to write this foreword to Mr John Vivian Hughes' republished monograph on Margam Castle.

We are moving into a new Millennium and a technological age but Margam still retains its special character - that feeling of space; that special sense of history; an environment that lifts the human spirit.

Any Local Authority can only be the custodian of Margam's heritage, and through the excellent work of the former West Glamorgan County Council, Margam Castle has been restored and protected, and the new Neath Port Talbot County Borough Council hopes to continue this work.

Recently plans have been announced for an Environmental Field Studies Centre for young people and adults at Margam, in partnership with the Field Studies Council, as well as a scheme to restore some of Margam's gardens to how they were in bygone days. It will take a variety of funding to achieve this aim but the new Authority has identified the way forward.

I am very pleased that the West Glamorgan Archives Committee has agreed to republish this important vignette of local history.

Ken Sawyers
Chief Executive
Neath Port Talbot County Borough Council
1998

The builder of Margam Castle: C. R. Mansel Talbot, M.P., F.R.S. (1803 - 1890)
Portrait by Sir George Hayter, 1834.

(Private Collection)

PREFACE AND ACKNOWLEDGEMENTS

Although the rambling early Victorian mansion we know as Margam Castle was built over 160 years ago, and suffered some thirty five years of sad neglect and vandalism after the second world war, like some very old and indomitable colossus, it still survives, presenting an air of romantic mystery and symbolism of a lost and great era of British history.

That it has done so, and still has a useful role to play, is in no uncertain measure due to the foresight and tenacity of the former West Glamorgan County Council and its inheritor authority of Neath Port Talbot County Borough Council. Many individual craftsmen have played an important part in its restoration, as indeed did their predecessors in its original construction. Tribute should also be paid to the late Lord Heycock, Councillor T.D.M.John, former Assistant County Architect Roy Harding and Park Director Ian Cadogan, for their personal direction and enthusiasm over the years.

It is sixteen years since the first edition of this monograph was published and pleasingly received by local people and admirers of Margam. For both the original and subsequent research on the Castle, I am indebted to many people who have provided advice and information. In particular, to D.John Adams, former Field Studies Officer at Margam Park. Also, to H.J.P. Arnold; H.Brooksby; Ian Cadogan; the late A.Leslie Evans; the late J.T.T.Fletcher; Roy Harding; Clive Johnstone; Sally Jones; the late C.P.M. Methuen-Campbell; the late Dowager Lady Mexborough; Arthur Rees; M.E.J. Rush.

For their generous permission to use the various photographs, acknowledgements are due to D. John Adams; Cardiff City Library; A.C.Cooper Ltd.; Barrie Flint; the National Library of Wales; Arthur Rees; South Wales Evening Post; and Peter Knowles, Port Talbot, whose several photographs and striking cover illustration are much appreciated.

Special thanks are also due to Miss Susan Beckley, County Archivist and the West Glamorgan Archives Committee for their support in publishing this new edition.

John Vivian Hughes
Port Talbot
May 1998

The North Front - Photograph taken May 1891 by Thomas Mansel Franklen. Note the original height of the side tower.
(Cardiff City Library)

When Thomas Mansel Talbot (1747 - 1813) decided to demolish the rambling and dilapidated old mansion of his Mansel ancestors at Margam in the late 18th century, he little realised the consequence of his actions. For although Margam was to be without a principal residence for the next fifty years, it did ensure that a grandiose country seat would eventually embellish the ancient and beautiful Margam Park estate. The old Mansel house was gradually demolished between 1787 and 1793, whilst much of its timber and stonework was re-used for the construction of the new orangery or stored for future use on the estate. The absence of a principal house here did not mean the complete abandonment of Margam with its superb Georgian Orangery and newly laid out pleasure gardens. Although T. M. Talbot was always to favour his estate at Penrice as his main residence, he did at one time consider building a classical mansion at Margam but never carried out any plans. For his own use he had retained an apartment at nearby Pyle Inn, whilst his later marriage and family ensured the use of a more modest but commodious house on the edge of the park known as Margam Cottage. The Talbot family frequently paid visits to Margam in the early 19th century, but it was with the coming-of-age of Christopher Rice Mansel Talbot[1] (1803-1890) that plans for a new house at Margam were to see fruition.

Even so it was still to be a few years before the young C. R. M. Talbot's inheritance and management of his estates enabled him to fulfil his dream. Proud of his ancient lineage, he was also greatly attracted to romantic Margam, and wished to build a suitable country seat which would compliment Margam's illustrious history. As early as 1828 he had confided his plans to his family, for in a letter of 7th December that year, his aunt, Lady Elisabeth Feilding at Lacock Abbey wrote to her son W. H, Fox Talbot: "Kit remained here a fortnight and went up to town with Mr. Feilding . . . Kit seems to like this place extremely and is determined to build a Tower to his new house & a large Hall like this & above all things *secret staircases!*"

In 1828 Talbot had the old parish road from Llangynwyd to Taibach diverted so as to avoid running through the new park. Following completion of this work, the agent Griffith Llewellyn of Baglan Hall, was able to carry out Talbot's instructions for other necessary preparations for the building of a new house. Indeed, preparations on a large scale were already under way, including the adequate drainage of the park. On October 12, 1829 a quarry was opened in the Great Park at Margam. Use was to be made of stone from quarries at both Margam and Pyle. In one of his early letters to Griffith Llewellyn, Talbot says, "I mentioned to your brother that I should be glad if any timber could be sold this winter from Landough or St. Mary Church besides which I want some cut at Margam for the use of the new buildings, such as for the purpose of making carts to fetch stone & other materials, beech or elm would suit as well as oak, but I must have a few oaks cut, say 8 or 10 trees which I leave to you to select, provided they are taken from the great wood or some place where they will not be missed."

The site chosen for the house was on an elevated position a few hundred yards up from the Chapter House ruins and Orangery pleasure ground, in the shade of the green slopes of Mynydd-y-Castell–itself the site of Margam's earliest habitation. A large force of workmen were employed to prepare and level the site. The new house would have a central position in a sylvan parkland setting, with views over the lush pastures of Margam to the sea. The young squire was determined that his new house would be the envy of the county and suited to his lineage, rank and fortune.

The agent Griffith Llewellyn and his brother Thomas were to be responsible for the general oversight of the building project, whilst the Margam bailiff, David Richards, became the effective Clerk of Works. Regular sums of money were paid by the Estates Office to the bailiff who would then pay the labourers. However, the stone masons and other craftsmen were paid directly by the agent. Many of the workmen and craftsmen employed on the new building were themselves the sons of men who had worked on the building of Margam Orangery for T. M. Talbot. There was always a sense of continuity with employees and their families on the Margam estate which lasted into the 20th century.

Precisely when and where Talbot encountered his future architect is not known. He appears to have cast around widely and considered several possible architects. One of his first choices was the eminent architect Robert Lugar (1773-1855). Lugar was a skilful practitioner of the picturesque and castellated Gothic mansions in the manner of John Nash. Author of several architectural books and sometime Surveyor of Essex, he had built numerous large country houses all over the country. In Wales he built Glanusk Park, Breconshire and Maesllwch Castle, Radnorshire. His most successful and famous building in Wales was Cyfarthfa Castle at Merthyr Tydfil for the Crawshay family. Probably it was this building, completed in 1825 that first drew Talbot's notice to Lugar. However, he does not appear to have met with Talbot's approval, as we see from a letter written early in 1830 from Talbot to Griffith Llewelyn: "That scoundrel Lugar has charged me £250 for *one* drawing, which I would not value at £5. It was his own proposal coming here, and he did not send his plans till after I decided on Hopper's. I intend to appeal to the law."

This is our first indication of Talbot's concern for the cost of everything and his choice of Hopper as his architect. Thomas Hopper (1776-1856) had become quite a fashionable architect since he had undertaken commissions for the Prince Regent (later George IV) at Carlton House, notably the addition of a large Gothic styled conservatory constructed of cast-iron. This royal patronage brought Hopper a large and fashionable practice as a country-house architect, where he built new or enlarged older houses in England, Scotland, Wales and Ireland. He was also County Surveyor of Essex and designed several buildings in that county, notably Danbury Park, begun in 1830 and bearing a strong resemblance to Margam, being in the same Tudor Gothic style. Hopper himself wrote: 'it is an architect's business to understand all styles and to be prejudiced in favour of none.' In fact Hopper seemed to prefer the Gothic style, but designed houses in the Norman, Tudor, Jacobean and Classical style. He was a most versatile architect who excelled in the principle of the picturesque. Some of his better known houses include Penrhyn Castle, Caernarvonshire; Llanover Court, Monmouthshire; Kinmel Park, Denbighshire; Gosford Castle, Co. Armagh; and works at Alton Towers, Staffordshire. Hopper also built many public buildings including the Atlas Fire Insurance Office, London; St. Mary's Hospital, Paddington; the Carlton Club, London; and Essex County Gaol. He also unsuccessfully submitted designs for the new Houses of Parliament in 1836.

Whilst Hopper is the recognised and accredited architect for Margam, it is rather interesting to find that another distinguished architect was closely involved with the building of Margam and almost certainly influenced the finished house with work on the interior and exterior, the stables, terraces and lodges. This was the Shrewsbury architect Edward Haycock (1790-1870), who had been a pupil of Sir Jeffry Wyatville, the famous architect of Windsor Castle. Haycock was the County Surveyor for Shropshire, designing and building numerous churches and country houses in Wales and the Border counties. In fact, Haycock was primarily regarded as a church architect, one of his early works being Holy Cross Church, a chapel-of-ease to Margam, built at Taibach in 1827. It seems likely that he had received this commission on account of his reputation as a church builder and following his design and building of Coedriglan, near Cardiff, the elegant home of the Rev. John Montgomery Traherne, who was a brother-in-law to C. R. M. Talbot. Coedriglan was built in the classical style between 1820 and 1821. A few years later Haycock built a superb classical mansion at Clytha, Monmouthshire in 1824-28. His involvement at Margam, where he was the supervisory architect, covered the years 1830 to 1840. During this period he was also responsible for the new lodges and rebuilding at Penllergaer, near Swansea in 1832-34 for C. R. M. Talbot's other brother-in-law, John Dillwyn Llewelyn. Haycock was also chosen for alterations and extensions to Penrice between 1840 and 1842, and may have been responsible for work carried out at Baglan Hall for Griffith Llewellyn about the same time. Another well-known house by Haycock is Glynlliffon, Caernarvonshire. Churches include Llanon, Carmarthenshire; St. David's, Carmarthen; St. Michael's, Aberystwyth; public buildings include the Butter Market and other buildings in Shrewsbury, and the Market Hall, Dowlais. He appears to have been quite a prolific architect with a busy and wide practice. It is therefore all the more surprising that he spent so much time at Margam, never having been properly credited with the work he did there.

Thus, we have two distinguished 19th century architects involved with Margam. However, there is a third person who was to greatly influence the architectural style and finished designs at Margam. This was C. R. M. Talbot himself. Certainly, Talbot, and many other 19th century squires were to be influenced by their own particular heritage, and the re-awakening and fashionable interest in antiquarian matters, gothic romance and medieval pageantry, which was to culminate in the great Gothic Revival which stayed for so much of Victoria's reign. In Talbot's case, we also have other important considerations. He was greatly influenced by the stately architecture of two family homes. Firstly, Lacock Abbey in Wiltshire, ancestral home of the Talbot's and residence of his cousin, W. H. Fox Talbot; and secondly, Melbury House in Dorset, the seat of his mother's family, the Fox-Strangways, Earls of Ilchester. Lacock Abbey was formerly a convent, whose buildings and lands were acquired in 1540 by the Sharrington family (ancestors of the Talbots) who retained much of the original abbey buildings through succeeding generations. The original buildings were further embellished in 1754-56 by John Ivory Talbot, who built an impressive entrance arch and large entrance hall in the fashionable Gothic style to the designs of the architect Sanderson Miller. Thus, the tall twisted chimneys, Gothic and Tudor windows, towers and pinnacles of Lacock all served to stimulate Talbot's taste for the picturesque and the romantic. Melbury had been acquired by the Strangways family in 1500, and incorporated a Tudor house with later 17th and 18th century additions. The focal point of Melbury was its 16th century lantern tower, hexagonal shaped, rising from the centre of the house. This feature was to be the inspiration for the larger octagonal tower eventually built at Margam. Talbot's fascination for architecture was obviously shaped in his early years on visits to these family homes. Margam was therefore really designed by three men Hopper, Haycock and Talbot; and influenced by two earlier houses–Lacock and Melbury, whilst eventually presenting a unique creation in sympathy with its sylvan surroundings, evocative of a rich and illustrious past–which was exactly what C. R. M. Talbot had in mind.

Sadly, no finished elevations, drawings or plans exist for Margam, with the exception of three small rough sketches. Two of these are rough pencil plans by

The north and west fronts in 1889. Photograph by A. McKinnon
(*Cardiff City Library*)

Hopper, which show the ground floor plan of the house very much as finally built. The major difference between the two plans is in the siting of the main staircase in the centre of the house. In one plan the bottom of the staircase is shown facing north and the doors into the entrance hall. whilst the second plan shows the executed design with the staircase facing west into the centre of the inner hall. Another interesting little pen and ink sketch shows a crosssection of the Staircase Hall and Tower, with lofty Gothic arches, plaster ceiling pendants, balustrades, and the arch at the head of the staircase. Interestingly, this drawing shows a slightly different design arch from that executed. The drawing shows an ordinary Tudor arch with squared-off hood moulding and spandrels, whilst the final work depicted an elaborate ogee arch surmounted with a finial and with crocketed pinnacles either side, possibly modelled on Sanderson Miller's Gothic arch at the entrance to Lacock's forecourt. One other surviving plan is a ground-floor plan of a portion of the domestic offices and back staircase. The fact that it has not been possible to trace any further drawings or plans of Margam does not mean that there were none. We know that Hopper did present Talbot with detailed elevations and plans, and probably Haycock would have completed some drawings too. Many of these architectural drawings were later framed and hung in the corridors at Margam until their disappearance in 1941.

The style chosen for the mansion was Tudor Gothic and Hopper was to excel himself with this style at Margam. Encouraged by Talbot, he gave free reign to his imagination, so that the final result would be a sea of towers, turrets, pinnacles, cupolas, battlements and gables. Margam was to be as highly romantic as any Gothic enthusiast could possibly wish or dream.

A series of letters and extracts from the estate accounts for 1830 to 1840 help to give us a better picture of the building of the mansion, referred to as the "new house" or the "great house", before its successive labels of Margam Park, Margam Abbey and Margam Castle were in use.

Running totals of the expenses incurred were meticulously kept in the estate accounts by the agent. Between 1830 and 1832 these accounts record payments of almost £8,000 for wages, materials, freight and haulage charge. Of this, £4,286. 1s. 7d was paid out for the year 1831 alone. There was a great flurry of activity on the estate as ships arrived at the harbours of Taibach and Aberavon. These ships carried limestone from Aberthaw, lead from Gloucester, slate from Cornwall, and glass from Liverpool. Newly built wagons hauled stone from the local quarries, timber from the estate plantations, and various cargoes unloaded at the local ports.

The accounts for 1830 record £55. 0s. 7d paid in March to James Prichard, brickman, for raising clay and making bricks at Margam. In a letter to his agent written at Melbury on March 6, Talbot remarks: "I believe I shall not employ Gubbins to saw the stone only to raise it ... I find from Haycock that the kiln is usually built for the brickmaker, but not the sheds." Griffith Llewellyn had already investigated the practicability and expense of making bricks and procuring sand locally, and large quantities of bricks were supplied from a new kiln at Margam. The site of the kiln gave rise to the later name of Brickyard plantation. The new building account shows that in May 1830 the mason, David Williams was paid £14. 3s. 0d for building a brick kiln at Margam. The total for repairing the road in the Great Park, loading stone at Pyle and burning lime at Taibach came to £88 3s. 6d.

Earlier, on April 15th, Talbot sent another letter to Llewellyn:

Fentons Hotel St. James's
London April 15, 1830

Dear Sir,
    I cannot tell the exact date of my sisters marriage, but I think probably the 28th inst.
    The lead is at Saml. Oakley's wharf Gloucester, & Haycock will desire him to deliver it.
    I had rather you would defer selling the other lot of timber till I come down, as I must come in a week or two to arrange the foundation of the house.
    I have got a better elevation than ever now. I am sorry Richards is so ill. I think he would not have been so much afflicted by the accusations of dishonesty if he saw the affair in its right light. I told his son in law to tell him that if dishonesty had been proved against him, I would not have kept him a day in my service; & that I punished him for rendering a false account of labourers time, only.
    I had always intended to return him the money stopped, if nothing was proved.

I am Dear Sir,

Truly Yours,

C. R. M. Talbot

The letter is interesting from two points. It shows Talbot was still querying every payment and scrutinising the accounts thoroughly. He appears at this time to have doubted the actions of his bailiff David Richards in some matter. Also, he indicated his intention to visit Margam to see the foundations being laid. A further letter from Talbot dated 23rd April states:

"Mr. Haycock will be down at Margam on Thursday. and I have to beg you will furnish him with twelve labourers to be employed in levelling & digging the foundations for the new house. Pyle quarry should be further cleared as regards the stratum of earth on top, much of which being marle, I should think the farmers would be glad to have spread over the fields. I have concluded a bargain with Haycock. He is also to have a bed at the cottage, till he can provide himself with a lodging. I have given him leave to fit up the old summer-house as a residence for his workmen. I have also stipulated he shall employ no workmen but whom I appoint, excepting for setting & cutting the stone, that being work for which first-rate artificers must be procured. I hope you shall give him every facility in the outset. I believe I shall get my timber at 2s per foot which will be a great saving."

Writing from London a few weeks later on May 19th he informs Llewellyn that:

"The contract with Haycock is not yet completed, but you shall have a copy of the specification in a day or two. When you mention the sum of £177 and building the keepers house besides the excavations for cellars & foundations. Observe, I only find rough timber & rough stones for Haycock's workmen's cottages, he is to pay the carriage & all other expenses attending their erection. The following are my ideas with regard to the carriage & no. of horses required. Two teams of horses from Pyle Quarry making each two journeys will deposit 12 tons of stone per day, and will

finish the whole 3125 tons in 260 days, or less than 1 year. I calculated the carriage of stone at 4s per ton, & I think by employing 2 teams of my own at this work, I shall do it for less than £625 and then the horses can be employed for other purposes after the 1st year. One team of my own must be employed in carting rough stone, brick & sand. In all say ten horses. As for lime, for the first year I must pay the tenants for bringing it, for you must recollect it is only summer's work, & I should have nothing to employ the horses in winter. Lead & timber will not be immediately wanted & you may exercise your discretion in buying cart-horses, I should like Powell to buy. My eldest sister talked of going to Margam to lay the first stone of the building, but perhaps now she is at Penrice she may not like to come over. Will you let her know & if she does not come, you may lay the first stone & see the workmen get the usual treat. It is of importance that the stone should be brought from Pyle soon, on accord of its drying. D. Richards time will only be required occasionally after the workmen have done excavating. Had you better not agree with Gubbins to raise stone at per ton, or per foot if he will do it for 2s I will accept."

An interesting postscript says "In case of you being short of money, I can remit, but I shall require to see by your books, that, we have as balance on hand."

Talbot's active interest in every aspect of the building activities and cost shows itself again in a letter of the 7th June:

"I enclose a letter from Jenkin Rees and have been advised by the leading brokers in the city to take his offer it being below the present market price. You may therefore tell him I will take 100 loads by way of sample but it must be delivered at Taybach this year. Don't you think he asks too much for the carriage to Margam? 2s a foot comes to 8s. 4d per load or 16s per journey. Hopper is very angry they have abandoned the quarry at Pen y Castel. You are going to much greater expense than is needed for rough stone, I know the stone in the great wood and graig goch is better than that which is nearer, but that on Pen y Castel is good enough, only that it is more expensive and less showy for Haycock, for the same reason Aberthaw lime is a most needless expense, except for the tower ... Remember Haycock is to pay all expenses attending workmens houses. I find only rough stones and timber."

He later appears to query the account rendered by a local haulier, Jenkin Rees of Taibach, in a further letter to the agent:

These are the following objections to Jenkin Rees' bill.

1. *He has sent 253 deals and I ordered only 200.*
2. *He has charged ⅔ crown and ⅓ midling whereas I ordered ½ & ½. However I am willing to pay accordingly as it really is one or the other, but I cannot take Jenkin Rees's dictum as to which is which. Haycock & Hopper will be shortly here and they shall say.*
3. *It is not certified by Shurmer or Richards that the quantity charged has been delivered, this you will please to insist on in all cases, especially as I put Shurmer for the express purpose of measuring the materials & seeing there is no waste.*

I have no objection to pay him £200 in part, without prejudice to my claim to dispute the bill as it now stands, at least till the arrival of my architect."

Whether Talbot or his family were at Margam later that month to see the foundations of the new house being laid is not certain. The ceremony is recorded in the estate accounts for June 17th when Margaret Betterton "for dinner and beer for

167 men and 9 boys given at the laying down of the foundation stone of new building at Margam" was paid the sum of £17. 3s. 0d. Mrs. Betterton and her husband kept the Corner House Inn at old Margam village. During his stays in South Wales, Talbot usually resided at Penrice, but writing from there on 27th June he tells Llewellyn: "I hope to be at Margam on Thursday, therefore beg you to tell Kitty to prepare the cottage. I expect Mr. Hopper on the 30th." Talbot's reference to the cottage is to Margam Cottage, which he and his architects stayed at during their frequent visits to Margam.

Further entries in the accounts for June 27 record "John Shurmer, superintendent quarrying stone digging foundations and drains" was paid 84 guineas, whilst a shipment of lead from Gloucester was received on the 28th. Talbot's business acumen and grasp of mathematics comes to the fore once again in one of his last letters of 1830 dated 9 October:

"For your guidance, I beg to mention that the quantity of stone supplied by Mr. Gubbins from the beginning of the working up to the 9th October 1830 is 18603 feet for which at 2½s per foot, he is entitled to the sum of £193. 15s.7½d. The number of bricks supplied by the brickmaker to the same day, is 110,000 for which he is entitled to £73, but I believe that he has to the value of £120 now lying in the brick yard ready made & burnt, so that if he has drawn as much as £200 he is not much over the mark."

Some entries for the year 1831 give an interesting insight into the range of activities and costs involved, as well as providing names of some of the artisans employed:

June 14
 Francis Lewis of Neath for 9750 bricks at £2 per thousand £19 10s 0d

June 20
 John Jones for raising and squaring 512 yds of flagstones at
 Havod Quarry at 1s per yard £25 12s 0d

June 24
 James Pritchard for making bricks at Margam also £22-16-4d
 excise duty £114 6s 3d

June 29
 Jenkin Rees Taibach for 1031 ft of Deal 2s 5½ per ft £125 14s 3d

Sept 6
 Freight of 41 tons of slate from Bocastle to Taibach £9 4s 6d

Sept 30
 Freight of 47 tons of slate from Bocastle to Taibach £10 11s 6d

Nov 2
 Mr. Bryant for 400 red bricks at 35s ton £7 0s 0d

Writing on the 19th August 1831 Talbot refers to the use of deals in other building work on the estate saying: "Mr. Hopper is of opinion that Welsh deal is as good as most of the American sent to this country. The roof should therefore be of Welsh deal for the barn at Cwrt y Defaid." Another interesting statement shows in a letter of 1 November notes " . . . I have strictly examined Shurmer as to the bricks, and the result is in round numbers, that Pritchard has sent to the building 510,000 bricks & 10,000 tiles." The total sum spent on the building by November 1831 was £4,286 1s 7d for the preceding year.

Talbot provides an interesting insight into the stage of developments at Margam with a letter to his cousin W. H. Fox Talbot dated 14th December 1831:

"My house is roofed in and though I say it, most superbly executed. I am curious to see your gallery, but that must be deferred till another opportunity, I hope your builder has satisfied you as mine has me. I am going to make a terrace 130 feet wide with a pierced quatre-foil parapet and flights of steps and I have a new design for a tower, most gorgeous to behold."

Under the heading "New Building", the estate accounts for 1832 record a few more interesting snippets of information:

March 26
    Benjamin Howell Neath for Hair for plaster £17 16s 0d
    Neath for Hair Cowbridge for Laths

July 17
    William Gubbins 4902 ft of stone at Pyle, Clearing rough rock
    1568 yd 14 ft £124 10s 0d

July 16
    New Stables

Sept
    Freight of Lead Gloucester to Swansea

The reference to hair for plaster reminds us that in the 19th century horse hair was frequently used as a binding agency when mixing plaster. From these entries, it would appear that work had begun on the new stables, probably the first stable to be built was the large building[2] to the south east of the mansion, approached from both the terrace and stable yard.

Two of the entries for 1833 refer to the building of the terrace wall:

May 20
    Mason building terrace wall £15 7s 6d

Oct 23
    Rees Jones mason 172 perches terrace wall 2s 8d per 32 feet
    quar stone 8d per ft £24 0s 0d

The terrace walls to the south of the mansion were low battlements, with small pillars at regular intervals, dropping several feet. to the level of the parkland. The terrace walling at the south-west corner of the terrace had a higher, more decorative stonework topped by elongated battlements with a pierced screen of stone blocks of quatre-foil design. The terrace walling at the south-west corner of the terrace had a carved stone dragon in the corner surmounting the low wall. A highly decorative pierced screen of Gothic stone tracery continued at a greater height around the north side of the terrace, connected to the north-west corner of the house with a matching

The south front and stables. Photograph taken by Thomas Mansel Franklen, May 1891.
(Cardiff City Library)

traceried wooden door. This elaborate screen is broken at intervals by upright sections of stonework containing niches, capped with small cupolas, part of the screen forming a stepped bay. The whole screen was surmounted by Gothic finials and fleur-de-lis in stone. It remains one of the most decorative features of the castle exterior.

The year 1834 sees further developments at Margam, recorded thus in the estate accounts:

June 20
Freight of lead-glass of Margam packet £4 3s 0d

July 22
Freight of 15 boxes glass from Liverpool to Swansea £4 0s 0d

Sept 8
Opening quarry on Castle Hill

Oct 20
2 small parcels for Mr. Hopper

Nov 3
Drain from Brewhouse to main

Nov 8
Lead from Gloucester

Nov 22
Glass on Elizabeth from London to Swansea

Dec 29
Penarth for Alabaster

The brewhouse referred to, was actually concealed in a large tower structure at the north east corner of the castle yard. The year 1834 saw great advances towards the completion of the house, with work on the domestic offices and outbuildings competing with the work being carried out on the interior of the main house, where an army of plasterers, carpenters and painters were busily at work. Writing to Griffith Llewellyn from London on March 16th 1834, Talbot advises him that: "Three chimney pieces are shipped in the Enterprise, Captain Roberts, for Swansea, to sail Sunday for me. Richard Walters of Swansea the agent. As soon as they arrive, send one of my wagons for them and desire Haycock to fix them in the North West bedroom, the middle bedroom on the West Front, and the middle bedroom on the South front."

Estate records for the year 1835 show: " . . . masons putting up coccle, plasterers making flue in alabaster houses" on January 26th, whilst April 20th saw the digging of further foundations for domestic offices, levelling ground on west front of house on May 18th, and payment of £133 to "Mr. C. Bowler, carver for work done on Great House 7 weeks at £5 per week, 14 weeks at £7 per week." It would be interesting to know precisely what carving Mr. Bowler was responsible for in the house. There was to be an abundance of carving on door frames, pediments, panelling, friezes and mouldings in all the main reception rooms. An entry for June 29th records the building of the dairy, whilst the period July to September saw further work on the dairy, brewhouse and other domestic offices ranged around the

Margam Park. The seat of C. R. M. Talbot Esqr. M.P.

The Mansion from the South East. A little known engraving published by E.S.&A. Robinson of Bristol c.1885

(*Author's Collection*)

courtyards. November saw continuation of work on the walling of the terrace. The new house and its environs positively teemed with activity as a completion date appeared nearer and nearer.

By 1836 most of the work on the interior of the main house was complete, although work still continued on some of the domestic offices and outbuildings. The records continue to give details of work being carried out such as flagging the dairy and plastering the brewhouse, whilst superintendent John Cadman was paying £50 a time to various craftsmen at the Castle for work completed.

1837 saw continued activity, with plasterers still at work, walling in the passage and wine cellar being attended to, whilst the carpenters were employed throughout the year on various jobs in the house. Foundations were dug for additional stables to the east of the house. Talbot must have been well pleased with the progress and his almost finished house, still keeping an active interest on every matter. One terse message in December 1838 said "Cadman has no business to give any orders for work inside the house at Margam." Foundations for stables and coach house were dug in June of that year and work was in progress on a new road up to the house.

In March 1839 Lady Mary Cole (Talbot's mother) wrote to her nephew Henry Fox Talbot from Margam: " . . . as usual there are a great many people employed–they are levelling & sloping the ground behind the house & making steps from the terrace down to the gardens but it will be long before they make much shew, the space is so great that the people look like ants making their nest tho' not near so diligent." Work continued on the outbuildings, the laundry and coach house were completed, whilst the records show payment of £48 for 6,000 slates used on some of the courtyard outbuildings.

The new house at Margam must have been a truly, wonderful sight to its proud owner as completion of the work came near. The cost had been well over £50,000–the equivalent of several million pounds today, but this still does not take into account the vast resources which a great estate like Margam contributed to such a project. The house was basically built around a complex of three courtyards, forming an oblong site, with four elevations, three of which included the most decorated parts of the main house. The mansion is mostly built of local sandstone, which has mellowed beautifully over the years. Inside, use was made of a harder stone for the staircase hall, whilst bricks were used extensively for interior walls, the cellars and other parts of the building. Oak and pine was used for rafters and flooring, with an ingenious use of cast iron railway lines to support and strengthen the stone landings of the main staircase. Elsewhere cast iron was used for the drainage system, for grilles and ventilation covers. The guttering and water pipes were of lead, with the Talbot crest embellishing each drip box above the downpipes. The complicated roofing system was of lead and Cornish slate. Indeed the roof was constructed at so many levels and angles it was always to be necessary for a small army of men to regularly sweep out the gutters and gulleys, whilst the onset of snow saw estate workmen sweeping the roofs clean. The great number of elaborate chimney stacks, all in variations of the Tudor style, were especially made in Bedfordshire and brought to Margam.

The North or main entrance front faced towards Mynydd-y-Castell, starting with stables and other out-buildings at its north easterly corner, with stone pillars surmounted by the Heraldic Lion of the Talbot's, leading into a cobbled courtyard. This elevation continued around a large square tower which concealed the brewery, along a length of battlemented wall to a huge castellated gate-way and arch,

The Mansel coat-of-arms on the Octagonal Tower.
(Peter Knowles, Port Talbot)

The famous Palladium Stone in the South Facade.
(Peter Knowles, Port Talbot)

surmounted by a shield bearing the arms of the Mansel Talbot family. This gate-way opened into the main courtyard and the entrance to the kitchens and domestic offices. Then came the main body of the house which contained part of the domestic quarters including the Servants Hall and the Housekeepers rooms on the ground-floor, with a self contained wing named the Bachelors Wing above on two floors. A small turret jutted out, with one high window having a hood moulding with carved stone dripstones in the shape of faces representing Sir Rice Mansel and Rev. Thomas Talbot, the first Mansel and first Talbot respectively to own Margam. The North elevation continued with the large entrance hall jutting out at right angles to the building, lit by two large stained glass windows, one in the east wall, and one high above the entrance arch. The entrance itself was flanked by soaring buttresses capped with tall Tudor pinnacles. The Tudor arch of the doorway, surmounted by the arms of Talbot and Butler, the arms of C. R. M. Talbot and his wife Lady Charlotte Butler, whom he had married in 1835. In the spandrels of the arch were stone shields bearing the letters M & T for Mansel and Talbot. This frontage continued with the blind North wall of the Library wing, whose chimney flues protruded from the wall, decorated on several levels with recessed coats-of-arms set in Gothic panels, topped by four of the tall Tudor chimneys.

The Western elevation was reached through the decorative pierced stone screen, This frontage was broken by pinnacle capped buttresses at the angles of the building, two double bays and one centre double bay which was flanked by two further smaller shaped bays, all with battlemented tops. The two small bays either side of the centre bay were in turn capped with ornate Gothic cupolas similar to those seen on the main front at Lacock. Below each cupola was a wide band of stonework decorated by coats-of-arms. A single gable with a shield was above the centre bay, whilst below the battlements the line of a moulding was broken at intervals by carved stonework of foliage and gargoyles. the latter also to be seen at the angles of the building. On the first floor level, two blind or dummy windows were inserted to make a more symetrical facade. A wide terrace in front of this facade led down broad stone steps to the Broad Walk, the Orangery gardens and ruins of the old abbey.

The South facade had a long elevation, like the North front, with the main house at the south west corner of the complex. There are two more double bays, followed by a slightly projecting wing which contained French windows with a small Oriel window above them. The whole south front, gabled or battlemented, is decorated with gargoyles and shields. An interesting small carved stone was set above the French windows. According to a manuscript written by the Rev. William Thomas of Baglan in 1787 this was " .. . supposed to be the Palladium Stone which a traditionary prophecy mentions as a stone that must be employed in the re-building of Margam in order to secure the prosperity of the house and which tho' lost for a time would be discovered again for that purpose."This account bears a further note in the hand of Rev. J, M. Traherne stating that this stone was "inserted over the door in South front of new house." It is difficult to actually make out the device on this time worn stone, but it is certainly an intriguing feature. An oriel window was set above this. The south front continued with a small tower at the corner of this projecting wing, the ground level having windows, with blank panels on the second and third floor level, whilst the band of stone at the bottom of the third level has most interesting hooded faces of monks carved in stone at each angle of the turret. The whole structure was surmounted by an elaborate pagoda shape cupola of pierced arches, topped with gargoyles of grotesque faces at each angle. This elevation continued with another door which lead from the Business room straight onto the

Shield bearing the De Clare Arms. Formerly part of the old abbey and later inserted into the east end of the Castle Stables.
(D. John Adams, Port Talbot)

Carved Dragon
on the West Terrace.
(Peter Knowles, Port Talbot)

terrace. The south front continued with more Tudor windows followed by a chimney breast decorated with further heraldic shields, continuing up to an unusual niche or arbour at the south east corner, set under an arch surmounted by Gothic pinnacles. The line of the building continued with the first stable block to be built (now the Interpretative Centre, and during the period 1930-41 a Squash Court and garage) and on into the stable yard. The eastern side of the castle contained the stables, coach-house and other outbuildings around a courtyard.

The kitchens and domestic offices were grouped around two other court-yards, whilst an inner courtyard was situated in the centre of the main house. Dominating the whole complex was the lofty Octagonal Tower with its tall mullioned windows lighting the main staircase below, and a windowed viewing room or sun lounge at the top. Below these windows on the north and south sides, was the coat-of-arms of the Mansels. A battlemented parapet on top of the tower was reached by means of a spiral staircase contained in a smaller tower which rose alongside the octagonal tower. This smaller tower had heightened merlons whose stonework rose several feet above the level of the pinnacles and weather vanes on the main tower. This extra stonework was removed c. 1957, so that the present level is not the original. A stone moulding below the battlement line of this small tower includes numerous carved heads.

The visual effect of the whole building is both impressive and romantic. Turrets and gables vie with Tudor chimneys, pinnacles and cupolas, to present a fascinating sky-line. Bay and oriel windows break the facades of the house together with other windows of every possible size and shape. The owner's pride in family history is amply reflected in the great number of shields and coats-of arms of various branches of the Mansel Talbot family which appear on the stonework. In addition, older pieces of stonework and carvings from the old Mansel house and Abbey were incorporated into the new building as dripstones or placed on other mouldings. One can be identified from a manuscript note by the Rev. J. M. Traherne who wrote: "When the roof of that part of the cloisters abutting on the Chapter house was repaired in 1836, an ornamented cross was found lying on the top, with a shield in its centre, bearing 3 chevrons probably the Clare arms. Doubtless this fragment adorned part of the groined roof of the Abbey Church. It has recently been inserted in the Eastern gable of the new stables at Margam." This can still be seen above the entrance into the present Interpretative Centre.

It was natural that both during and after the building of so large and magnificent a house as Margam, that the interest of local people and visitors should be greatly stimulated, so that they would pay visits to see the new house. In his diary for Friday 27th May 1831 Lewis Weston Dillwyn, M.P., friend and ally of Talbot, records: "In the morning Talbot took me to see his new palace." The local gentry and their guests often made up parties to visit Margam, as can be seen from 'A Journal of a Trip to Glamorganshire' by Esther Phillips Williams of Cowley Grove, Oxon.:

Monday, July 17th 1836 ... After Dinner we formed a party to visit Margam Abbey and House. Some were mounted on nags, and others proceeded in my brother Benjamin's phaeton ... The Abbey and the ground on which it stands are the property of Mr. Talbot, the squire of the place, who is now building a splendid mansion in sight of the ruin. We remarked that there was a great similarity of style between this building and the new part of Windsor Castle, but we found afterwards that Wyattville was the architect of both.

The Entrance Hall following its restoration and official opening in 1992.
(South Wales Evening Post)

The most splendid part of the interior was the staircase and landing place. Many of the rooms were handsome, and the style of fitting them up all different. The garden too, is quite in keeping with the house and may boast some rare flowers."

Of course, Wyatville was not involved at Margam, but possibly the fact that Hopper had carried out work for George IV or that Haycock was a former pupil of Wyatville might have confused the identity of the architect. In any event, it remains an interesting contemporary account of Margam. Visiting country houses or stately homes by the middle classes or gentry was not unusual in the 19th century and is by no means a modern pastime. Naturally, many owners had mixed feelings on the subject and most owners forbade such intrusions on their privacy. Surprisingly, Talbot did not at first object to such visits, but his views are clearly expressed in a number of letters to Griffith Llewellyn:

40 Belgrave Square
London, May 11th 1839

Dear Sir,

It is my wish, though I have not made any order on the subject, that the house at Margam should not be indiscriminately shewn. Very great inconvenience is the consequence of parties of 20 or 30 persons going over to walk around the house not as much to gratify curiosity, as to make parties. I allowed the house to be seen indiscriminately while building, but now it is finished, serious damage to the furniture would be the consequence of allowing large parties to roam about inside. You are very welcome to show it to any friends who may wish to see it.

Yours truly,

C. R. M. Talbot

In another letter a few weeks later, whilst querying some management problems, he speaks further on the subject:

40 Belgrave Square
May 24 1839

Dear Sir,

Lady Charlotte heard from Mrs. Meade this morning and she mentions among other things that Cadman had been away for ten days, and that Bray has also frequently absented himself, insomuch that John Roberts had complained that he was frequently without work to do, for want of orders. I wish to know if these absences are duly accounted for in your payments to Cadman, & if he keeps Bray's time as well as the masons,

She also says that Cadman had sent you the other day when you were in the village, to tell you she had gone out from the house, and that in consequence, you came up to the house, and delivered a message to the housemaid to the effect that she was not to shew the house any more. I wish to know the truth of this.

Yours very truly,

C. R. M. Talbot

The Gothic Fireplace and replica panelling in the Entrance Hall.
(Arthur Rees, Port Talbot)

Doors leading from the Entrance Hall into the Staircase Hall. The Gothic Stalls are seen to the right of the doors.
(Peter Knowles, Port Talbot)

Poor old Griffith Llewellyn appears to have had something of a problem in pleasing his master and interpreting his exact wishes, as the following letter shows:

London
Dear Sir, *May 25th 1839*

I thought I had made myself clearly understood about the shewing of Margam. But as it seems I did not, I now beg you to understand that it is probable I may put a stop to the shewing without a written order, but that I make no order upon the subject at present, and will thank you immediately to convey a message to Mrs. Meade to the effect that your first message was a mistake.

Yours very truly,

C. R. M. Talbot

Later that same month, Talbot is still concerned about the work of Cadman, estate accounts and the showing of the house to visitors:

40 Belgrave Square
Dear Sir, *May 31st 1839*

It is advisable that you should speak to Cadman relative to his drawing his money during the time he was absent. If that time was as much as ten days, I certainly think he ought not to be paid, but should wish to know how he accounts for having charged his time before I find fault.

Regarding Bray & Roberts, I see that their time has been invariably entered in your accounts as under the head of "repairs". As there is a separate heading of "Expenses of the New building" I cannot conceive how this mistake which I have before noticed to you, comes to be repeated.

The reason that I inquired if Cadman had sent for you, is that Mrs. Meade has written to say, that Cadman had sent a message to you complaining of her absence and that there was no one to take care of the house. The poor woman will torment herself to death, I fear. As to shewing the house, it is my intention, for the reasons I have already given you, to discontinue doing so, but it would never do to commence such a discontinuance by desiring the housekeeper to refuse to shew it. When it becomes gradually known that the house is not shewn as a matter of course, I may then communicate my direction in a more positive form. But at present people would be greatly annoyed at being turned away from the door after coming a distance.

Yours very truly,

C. R. M. Talbot

Although work on the main house was virtually complete, Talbot still found many other matters which attracted his attention causing a flurry of letters and instructions to Llewellyn. Writing from Penrice on November 16, 1839 he says:

Sectional drawing of the Tower and Staircase Hall by Thomas Hopper.
(Author's Collection)

The Staircase Hall. Photographed by Spencer Nicholl, September 1885. Note the elaborate Victorian Gasoliers. The legs of the table in the centre were balusters from the staircase of the old Mansel House. *(National Library of Wales)*

The Staircase Hall. A photographn by Thomas Mansel Franklen, May 1891. Note the sculpture
from T. M. Talbot's collection and the Pipe Organ on the half-landing.
(Cardiff City Library)

"I certainly did not tell Cadman 'to apply to you for money on account of work he is now doing for Lady Mary Cole.' Firstly, because I do not believe he is doing any work for Lady Mary, and secondly because he never applied to me. When I last saw him, I asked him whether he had kept an account of what his men had been doing for Lady Mary and for Miss Talbot, separate from my account and whether he had applied the money drawn from you to the work to be done for Lady Mary and Miss Talbot, and I asked him in consequence of you having told me that he had drawn £25 per week which I knew could not be expended upon the work ordered to be done at Margam for me unless it includes items which I know nothing of, I wish to add that I consider part of your duty to make yourself acquainted with the details of these kinds of payments in my absence and that it is quite unsatisfactory to me to hear that Kent or Cadman have drawn such and such sums without any information from you as to the reasons for the increase.

The expense of making a culvert in the Little Park ought not to be included in the building account. It is part of the the repairs of the Estate. In reference to the raising of the labourers wages I certainly have no intention of raising daily wages. If any of my labourers wish higher pay they may go to the harbour which I shall begin upon next week.

Gravel's estimate for the embankment is considerably higher than what I should consider reasonable. I know not where in the world earth could be more cheaply moved than in that spot, all down hill no rocky ground, the bank close to the hollow and puddling on the spot. I know that the minimum price for embankments is 3d per yard and I think 4½d or 5d would be a good price for that one. As for the masonry at 10s 6d per perch it is ridiculous. I wish you would let Mrs. Meade know that we shall probably be at Margam next week."

The year 1840 sees work continuing at Margam as Talbot writing to his agent on the 3rd May, says:

"I send the following remarks for your guidance. Cadman is about leaving and Shurmer too old to do much good, it will be necessary for you therefore that William Jenkin should give more of his time to my affairs in the neighbourhood of the new building. His wage to be £1 1s per week, and his duties, to look after Bray and the joiners, W. David and carpenters. Shurmer and the labourers and the masons and plumbers.

The immediate business of the joiners is to fit up the stables and do certain work required in the house.

The carpenters are to make doors and windows for the new gardeners house, for the houses at Taibach and for two small cots to be built near the present smith's shop.

Masons to finish gardener's house as per contract, and to erect two small cots between those lately repaired and the plumbers by contract. Joiners to make a pair of gates for the stable yard and coach house doors. Also to prepare boarding of about 1½ inch thick and four feet long for lining the back stairs in the house, of lime tree.

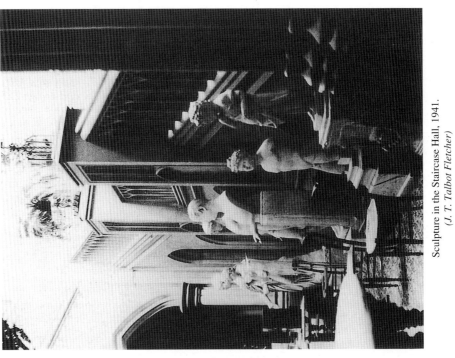

Sculpture in the Staircase Hall, 1941.
(*J. T. Talbot Fletcher*)

Head of the Main Staircase, 1941.
(*J. T. Talbot Fletcher*)

The Arch at the head of the Main Staircase, 1973. This leads to the Back Staircase. *(Arthur Rees, Port Talbot)*

The Great Staircase photographed in 1998. *(Arthur Rees, Port Talbot)*

The Great Staircase Tower and restored ceiling, 1992.
(South Wales Evening Post)

The Library looking north. Photographed by Spencer Nicholl, September 1885. Talbot had an extensive library containing many rare volumes. The door on the right led into the Staircase Hall.

(National Library of Wales)

The Library looking south. Photographed by Spencer Nicholl, September 1885. The door on the left led into the Staircase Hall, whilst the double doors in far wall opened into the Drawing Room. The Bay Windows looked out over the West terrace.

(National Library of Wales)

The Library, with the Van Dyck of Charles I and his family hung above the north fireplace.
(J. T. Talbot Fletcher)

The Library in 1942. The door on the right led into the Staircase Hall, whilst the windows
looked onto the Orangery Gardens.
(Author's Collection)

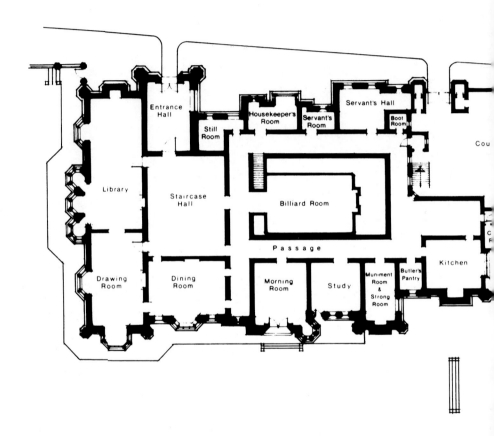

Entrance Hall

Still Room

Housekeeper's Room

Servant's Room

Servant's Hall

Boot Room

Cou

Library

Staircase Hall

Billiard Room

C F

Passage

Kitchen

Drawing Room

Dining Room

Morning Room

Study

Muniment Room & Strong Room

Butler's Pantry

A Plan compiled from information supplied by
Lady Mexborough (formerly Miss Josephine Talbot Fletcher)
and Mr. George Watson (formerly Capt. A. M. Talbot - Fletcher's chauffer)
February 1976

MARGAM CASTLE

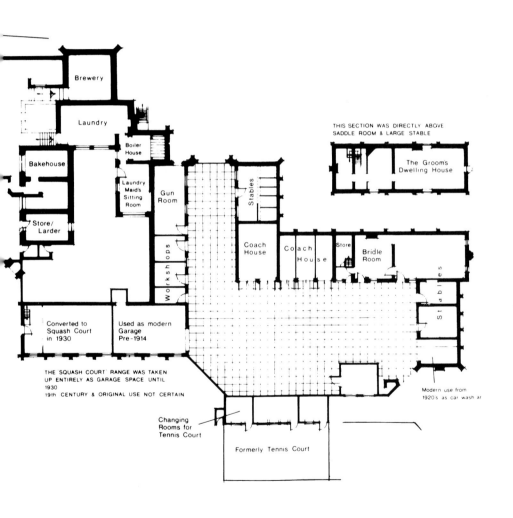

Brewery

Laundry

Boiler House

Bakehouse

Laundry Maid's Sitting Room

Gun Room

Store/ Larder

Workshops

Converted to Squash Court in 1930

Used as modern Garage Pre-1914

THE SQUASH COURT RANGE WAS TAKEN UP ENTIRELY AS GARAGE SPACE UNTIL 1930
19th CENTURY & ORIGINAL USE NOT CERTAIN

Stables

Coach House

Coach House

Store

Bridle Room

Stables

THIS SECTION WAS DIRECTLY ABOVE SADDLE ROOM & LARGE STABLE

The Grooms Dwelling House

Modern use from 1920's as car wash ar

Changing Rooms for Tennis Court

Formerly Tennis Court

The gutted Library in 1973.
(Peter Knowles, Port Talbot)

One of a pair of white marble fireplaces in the Library.
(Arthur Rees, Port Talbot)

The plumber is to paint the whole of the woodwork in the North row of bachelors rooms and passage, two coats, to paint the skirting in the bath room and deed room, to paint the whole of the walls and ceiling of the deed room and the skirting and doors of all offices, to glaze new cottage windows and paint hothouses.

The plasterer is to finish all plastering required in gardener's house as per yard contract and also such as remains unfinished in the stable."

Talbot's concern for every detail regarding the building and estate management in general is seen again in a letter sent from London on May 17th 1840:

"When I desired the paving of the stable yard to be completed, I alluded to the part of the stable yard which I had marked out as being paved. I do not think there was a week's work unfinished when I left. I said nothing about the flagging because it had better be deferred till I can superintend the laying of it. The stalls are not to be painted at all. I believe there was a sufficient quantity of plank, either of lime tree or deal, to finish the stalls of the five stall and four stall stable, which are the only ones I wish finished.

Poor old Shurmer's death will make a difference in my intention regarding William Jenkin. I think of giving him a house and 25 shillings a week and that he should devote all his time to the labourers and artificers at Margam.

I want the drains behind and before the stables kept open until I am satisfied they work properly and the same of the drains between the terrace and the gardens."

He continues in a letter of July 1st ". . . The work that I am most anxious about at Margam is the prosecution of the road forming the new eastern approach." The new road from the eastern approach was to be a long winding road, eventually leading to the stable yard and the north front of the mansion where it ended in a stately sweep before the main entrance. The eastern approach was used by Talbot as the main approach to the new house, and this remains so today, with the beautiful and impressive vista of the distant castle breaking upon the visitor's gaze as he approaches through the park. The eastern entrance consisted of a pair of plain iron gates, flanked by two stone pillars, each surmounted by the Talbot lion, but rather oddly facing inwards towards the park. One story is that Talbot had these heraldic beasts facing towards the house to watch over and protect the occupants of the castle. Indeed the position of these lions on the gate piers, and the siting of the two flanking lodges outside the gates, does tend to give one the impression that the whole entrance is sited the wrong way around.Usually entrance lodges are inside the gates and heraldic beasts face outwards. The two lodges, both in the Tudor style, but of slightly different design were probably designed by Haycock rather than Hopper. They are later than the main house and date from 1840-42. The approach to the castle was protected by two other lodges in a similar style, on the western approach to the estate. Middle Lodge was built alongside the road past the fishpond, whilst West Lodge occupied a prominent site near Groes village on the main road through Margam. West Lodge was sadly demolished with the destruction of Groes village in 1974 to make way for the new motorway.

A number of poems or englynion were written about the new Castle, when it became the subject given by the Rev. 0. Jenkins for the "Cadair Morgannwg"

The Dining Room. Photographed by Spencer Nicholl, September 1885. The door on the left led into the Drawing Room, whilst the door on the right led into the Staircase Hall.
(National Library of Wales)

The Dining Room looking east. Photographed by Spencer Nicholl, September 1885.
The doors led into a service corridor.
(National Library of Wales)

The Dining Room. A photograph taken by Thomas Mansel Franklen, May 1891. The door led into the Drawing Room. Note the paintings from Talbot's Art Collection. Over the door is Monamy's 'Shipping in a Calm', next is 'The Madonna and Child in Glory' by Veronese. Top right, 'The Rape of Ganymede' by Rubens, bottom right, 'A view of Westminster' by Canaletto.

(Cardiff City Library)

The Dining Room, 1941. The door on the left led into the Drawing Room, whilst the door on the right led into the Staircase Hall.
(J. T. Talbot Fletcher)

The Dining Room, 1998. The doorway on the right leads into the Drawing Room. The doorway into the Staircase Hall is blocked off.
(Arthur Rees, Port Talbot)

Eisteddfod in 1838. They were of course in Welsh and rather long, but a translation of one or two verses of the prize winning entry by Edward Williams 'Iolo Fardd Glas' (1770-1854), is given since they are of some contemporary and historical interest:

> We look to have an aspect–an ordered task
> Excellent and strange,
> From a splendid ruin, it holds its appearance
> Remembrance to be called a dwelling.
>
> The most splendid building in the province–A court of Monks
> A place above all destruction
> We will get a second loving look,
> In Margam a non-crooked work.

Talbot gives us insight into one of the problems likely to face the owner of a large house in the 19th century when he writes in June 1840: "I have a correspondence with the Board of Taxes about the window tax at Margam and they have agreed that no change is to be made until next year." Margam, with its many windows must have been something of a poser. Window tax was eventually abolished in 1851, no doubt to the great relief of many home owners. It is also interesting to note that the glass in the windows at Margam was a thick plate glass, often to be found in large houses of the period and offering a form of insulation.

Having described the exterior of the mansion and the continuing work on its environs, it is desirable to look at the interior in some detail. If the exterior was Tudor Gothic then the interior was Tudor Fantasy at its best with a few other styles thrown in for good measure. Both the Entrance Hall and the Staircase Hall were in the Gothic style, which was evident throughout the house with the notable exception of the library, drawing room, morning room and some bedrooms.

Entering the house through the main entrance, we would have passed through large double oak doors in a Tudor arch, into the Entrance Hall. This was large and impressive, giving a foretaste of the splendour of the interior. Some 31ft by 20ft, the floor was of black and white marble, with a repeat pattern of an abstract form of the Maunch or Sleeve from the Mansel coat-of-arms. Oak panelling up to a height of approximately 5 feet, surmounted by miniature crenellations, was ranged around the lower half of the walls. An intriguing aspect of this panelling was the reproduction in wood of architectural detail in the form of tall, slim flying buttresses capped by pinnacles, which were spaced at intervals around the panelling. The hall was lit by two large stained glass windows. One was a Gothic arch set with stained glass representing historical figures and knights, positioned above the main doorway. The second window was set in the east wall and contained heraldic stained glass representing 18 coats-of-arms of successive Mansel Talbot owners of Margam. A lofty apartment, rising the full height of the house, the entrance hall had a superb fan vaulted ceiling in plaster, with every Gothic detail picked out in ribs, bosses and pendants. Three large plaster pendants were suspended from the centre of the vaulting, with four plaster shields as central bosses facing north to south, each shield bearing a letter-C.R.M.T.-the builder's initials. To help light the hall, a large octagonal lantern was later suspended from the ceiling. On the west wall, in between the oak panelling was a superb Gothic fireplace of local quarella stone. This fireplace had a hearth with an ogee arch, surmounted by a finial and crenellations, with flanking pinnacles. The walls above the panelling were hung with large gilt-framed oil paintings, including a set of paintings by Hondecoeter. Italian and Flemish carved

The Dining Room fireplace, badly damaged in the 1977 fire.
(Arthur Rees, Port Talbot)

The Morning Room, with portrait of the four Talbot children above the fireplace, 1941.
(J. T. Talbot Fletcher)

walnut chairs were ranged around the hall, together with carved oak side tables and an oak circular centre table, with stand of Gothic arches surmounted by a veined grey marble top. A Persian carpet and 17th century oak chest completed the opulent furnishings.

A pair of double oak doors led from the Entrance Hall into the majestic Staircase Hall, which measured 46ft by 43ft. The doors themselves were set in an arched recess with carved pilasters and lintel, the spandrels containing the lion crest of the Talbots, the whole doorcase (matching the others in the inner hall) surmounted by miniature battlements or crenellations. The floor of the Staircase Hall was flagged, but covered with a carpet fitted to the sides of the hall, with a design of fleur-de-lys and riband trellis-work in pink on a rich brown ground. Huge pillars supporting the lofty Gothic arches occupied the centre spacing of the hall, being ranged around the majestic stone staircase, consisting of wide flights of steps, broken by a platform halfway up, leading to a half-landing and further flights of stairs and half-landings to the right and left. Hopper's surviving sketch shows a cross-section of the staircase hall, the arches and staircase. The staircase has stone balustrades of small narrow Gothic arches broken at intervals by squat stone pedestals surmounted by large candelabra. Immediately above the main staircase and supported by the high Gothic arches was the Octagonal Tower, whose large mullioned windows lit the staircase and the hall below. Standing on the staircase and looking upwards, it was possible to see a magnificent plaster ceiling of Gothic design with plaster pendant. Above this ceiling, reached by a winding staircase in the smaller side tower (accessible via the back staircase) was the sun room of the tower with superb views over the countryside and across the Channel. More elaborate plasterwork all richly gilded and painted, vaulted with pendants and bosses decorated with grotesque faces, could be seen on the lower ceiling around the arches of the hall. A later feature of the staircase hall was a superb set of fitted Gothic stalls or seats[4] built against the north wall, to the right of the hall doors. These stalls were elaborately carved, each stall seat having a panelled back with traceried woodwork set with the monograms of C. R. M. Talbot, his wife and children. The frieze above the tracery was carved with lifelike figures of squirrels, pheasants, rabbits, foxes and other animals and flowers. These stalls were inserted c. 1844 and besides being decorative, disguised part of the pipes of the central heating system which heated the main apartments. The stalls were matched with similar carved and traceried panelling on the north east wall, and to the left, of the hall doorway, continuing around the hall was more panelling.

C. R. M. Talbot brought most of his father's sculpture collection from the Orangery and placed it on either side of the main staircase. Antique and other busts and statues were arranged on plinths and pillars to decorate the hall. Richly carved Spanish walnut chairs, an oak bufret and cabinets, together with a pair of oak canopied seats of Gothic design, complemented the decor. Two other interesting pieces of furniture here, were a pair of circular tables with Charles II walnut baluster supports surmounted by a veined yellow marble top and a black marble top. The balusters were from the staircase of the old Mansel house, pieces of which had been salvaged and stored. Also in the hall was a chair weighing machine regularly used by Talbot.

From the Staircase Hall, access could be gained via a passage on the east side to the domestic offices and the Morning Room, Business and Muniment Room. Doors also lead off the hall into the Library, Drawing Room and Dining Room.

The Drawing Room. Photographed by Spencer Nicholl, September 1885. The Bay Window looked out over the West Terrace, whilst the double doors led into the Library. Note Miss Talbot's portrait by James Sant on far wall.

(National Library of Wales)

The Drawing Room. Photographed by Spencer Nicholl, September 1885. The doors led into the Library, Staircase Hall and Dining Room.
(National Library of Wales)

Panelling and plasterwork in the Billiard Room, 1973
(Arthur Rees, Port Talbot)

Carved Overmantel in the Billiard Room, 1973
(Arthur Rees, Port Talbot)

The Library was the longest and most spacious of the reception rooms, being 60ft by 24ft. Unlike most of the other rooms, the Library was in the Classical style with probably the best ceiling in the house, comprised of three deep oblong panels of richly moulded plaster with inner circles of garlands, and a wide deep cornice around the room. Gold leaf was extensively used on the library ceiling and other ceilings in the house. Lit by four of the bay windows of the west front, the library faced west with marvellous views down to the Orangery gardens. The door was a massive six panelled classical door with a pediment, although the other side, facing into the staircase hall, was of Tudor design. Carved white marble fireplaces, decorated in the classical style with acanthus were situated in the north wall and lower cast wall respectively. Ranged around the walls were large open bookcases, filled with Talbot's fine library including many rare books and fine bindings, numbering several thousand volumes covering the arts, literature, topography, history and science. Talbot was a great reader and a man of science, and the library was always his favourite room. One of the library's treasures was 'The Old English Chronicle of the 14th century', printed on vellum. Talbot's library rivalled those in other great country houses in Wales and was typical of collections owned by wealthy and learned 19th century gentlemen. The tops of the bookcases were decorated with a number of antique Roman busts. The walls of the library were hung in beige watered silk, replaced later in the century by a similar striped beige silk wall covering. Above the bookcases, ranged around the walls were many fine oil paintings bought by Talbot specially for Margam. Dominating the library was one of Talbot's proudest acquisitions, a huge canvas of Charles 1st, Henrietta Maria and their children after Van Dyck, Like most of the house, the library was furnished with a rich mixture of antique and contemporary furniture, including armchairs, sofas, side-tables, desks and writing-tables. Large Chinese porcelain vases, valuable Persian and Turkish carpets and other objects d'art completed this beautiful and cultured setting.

Double doors connected the south end of the library to the Dining Room which measured 40ft by 24ft. Doors also led from the Drawing Room to the Staircase Hall and the Dining Room. The Drawing Room was reputedly designed after one of the Salons at Versailles, certainly it was decorated in the French style of Louis Quinze, with an abundance of fine furniture in the Louis XV and Louis XVI styles. Fauteuils, side-tables, writing-tables, commodes, a grand piano and harp, all richly decorated with gilt, marquetry or boulle complemented the white and gold panelling of the walls and doors. The walls were decorated with French Rococco panelling set above the dado and chair rail, each panel hung with watered silk and edged with elaborate gilt carving. Above the doorcases were semi-circular panels carved in relief with flowers, foliage and emblems. whilst the egg and dart moulding of cornices were offset by the later addition of a wide frieze of shields and tiny pilasters. A crystal chandelier lit the room, reflected in a large carved gilt framed mirror above the Louis XV veined green marble fireplace. A Chinese lacquer screen, ormolu candelabra, porcelain vases and figurines completed the furnishings of this opulent room. The bays of the Drawing Room windows looked out onto the Orangery garden and terrace to the west, and the parkland and terrace to the south.

Doors from the staircase hall, serving passage and Drawing Room led into the Dining Room, which faced south over the terrace and park. This room measured 36ft by 25ft with a door into the Drawing Room in its west wall, into the staircase hall in the north wall, whilst a door connecting a serving passage was matched by another false door with shallow cupboard recess in the east wall. A bay window flanked by two smaller windows occupied the south wall. The floor had a wide surround of

The Billiard Room after the 1977 Fire.
(Peter Knowles, Port Talbot)

veined white marble with the plain centre covered by a richly coloured Kelim carpet. A handsome carved white marble fireplace was positioned in the north wall, arguably the finest in the castle, it was of Gothic design with twin turrets rising either side of a castellated centre piece, over the graceful Gothic arch of the hearth. The doors were Tudor in design with panels of Gothic arches. The ceiling of this room was of the finest plasterwork in an elaborate Gothic design, whilst the walls were hung in a rich red wall covering. Paintings from Talbot's art collection graced the walls in huge gilt frames. On the cast wall hung the large canvas 'The Story of Aristaeus' by Nicollo del Abbatte, whilst the west wall contained 'The Rape of Ganymede' by Rubens, 'The Madonna and Child in Glory' by Veronese, and Monamy's 'Shipping in a Calm', joined later in the century by Canaletto's study of Westminster. A large mahogany dining table and chairs, Georgian gilt sidetables, Italian gilt chairs and silver and gold brocade curtains created a fine setting for elegant meals. The silver plate used here was of considerable quality and quantity, comprising 18th and 19th century pieces, including dinner services, candelabra, trophies and dishes. Services of Sevres, Dresden, Minton, Worcester, Copeland and Coalport, together with Venetian and Irish glass and crystal made elegant place settings for the dining table.

Both the adjacent serving passage and a passage from the staircase hall gave access to the Morning Room. A favourite room of the family, this had doors leading off a passage and originally had a connecting door with the Business Room or study. This room was 23ft by 21ft and had French Windows leading onto the South Terrace. Its walls were covered in rich brocade and a large Victorian fireplace of grey marble was positioned in the west wall. The decorated plaster ceiling had a wide frieze of fruit and flowers. Above the fireplace hung a large gilt framed painting of the four Talbot children by E. L. Dubuffe, whilst smaller paintings were hung around the other walls. The room was furnished with many smaller and lighter pieces of furniture, including Chippendale, Adam and Regency pieces mixed with Victoriana.

Alongside the Morning Room was the Study or Business Room which measured 22½ft by 17ft and had a window and doorway leading onto the South Terrace. It was plainer and more functional than the other main rooms, with typical furniture of the period comprising bookcases, desk and chairs. A steel door led directly from this room into a small Muniment Room where shelves and boxes contained a vast amount of family and estate papers, including the famous Penrice and Margam Manuscripts. These included many old Abbey charters and the records and papers of the Mansel family. The room was used very much as an estate office until later in the century, hence the separate terrace entrance for use by visiting tenants or employees.

Continuing along the passage we would reach the Butler's Pantry and sitting room. The Butler's Pantry had a door leading directly into the Plate Safe. The heavy steel door was painted and disguised to look like an ordinary six panel door. Inside this safe, most of the valuables and silver plate was securely kept, an essential feature of large and remote country houses.

As might be expected in a great Victorian country house, with a large number of servants, the domestic offices were quite extensive with numerous rooms including the large kitchen with its huge oriel window looking onto the inner courtyard, scullery, still-room, steward's room, housemaids' sitting room, cook's sitting room, laundry, dairy, brewery, bakehouse, boot room, larders and numerous store rooms. Further store rooms and vast cellars were under the house, including a fine wine cellar. The outbuildings included a game larder, gun room, harness room, saddle

The Tapestry Bedroom, 1941
(J. T. Talbot Fletcher)

The Chinese Bedroom, 1941
(J. T. Talbot Fletcher)

room as well as coach house and stables. The North wing of the house contained the important housekeeper's room; with its large window it had a good view of the front entrance and arriving family or visitors. Also in this range was the Servants Hall looking out on the North approach. The back or servants staircase was sited in the middle of the house, opposite the north corridor and housekeeper's rooms. It rose behind the main staircase, and led to the servants' quarters, the tower room, the North or Bachelors Wing and the head of the main stairs. A smaller servants' staircase, a spiral one, was situated off a corridor on the south side of the house.

Continuing a tour of the main house, proceeding up the main staircase with its crimson carpet, the head of the stairs had an impressive Gothic doorway with an ogee arch and flanking crocketed pinnacles with a carved Gothic door leading to the back staircase. Flights of steps off the main staircase led to half landings either side, leading up to further flights to the main bedrooms on the first floor. A set of four 16th century Spanish panels in Petit Point, worked in coloured silks and silver thread, depicting historical scenes, were hung imposingly above the main staircase on the half-landings and stairs. Italian console tables and giltwood chairs, large mandarin vases and objects d'art lined the landings and main corridor. Also to be seen on a half-landing was a hand-manual pipe organ,[5] made for C. R. M. Talbot by Flight & Robson of London in 1834. It can be clearly seen in Mansel Franklen's photograph of the Staircase Hall in 1891. The richly carpeted stairs and landing led to suites of bedrooms and dressing rooms in the West and South Wings.

The west wing contained the Tapestry Bedroom, so called because its walls were hung with an exquisite set of four large 18th century panels of Brussels tapestry. These depicted 'The Feast of the Gods', the figures being worked into extensive landscapes woven in brilliant colours. The luxurious furnishings included a Flemish oak bedstead with spiral posts supporting an elaborately carved canopy. The curtains, headboards and canopy were of maroon and silver damask. A walnut table with marquetry, 17th century walnut chairs and a richly carved oak Flemish armoire were part of the remaining furnishings.

Leading off this bedroom was a Dressing Room in which was an elaborate Louis XVI gilt bedstead with panels of cream satin, embroidered with birds and flowers. Louis XV and mahogany furniture completed this room.

Probably the best remembered bedroom in the mansion was the fabulous Chinese Bedroom in the west wing. This style of decoration was a popular theme for a principal bedroom in great country houses of the 18th and 19th centuries. The walls were covered in hand-painted Chinese wallpaper depicting Chinese landscapes and figures of mandarins and dragons in brilliant colours. The room was furnished with beautiful pieces of chinoiserie, notably a bedstead painted cream and gold, with bamboo pattern posts and pagoda-shaped top and red silk hangings. Oriental vases and figurines, mahogany tables and Chinese chippendale chairs complemented the whole scheme.

The Green Bedroom took its name from this typical Victorian room's colour scheme, where a bedstead with painted green and gold posts, hung with red damask curtains, was matched with a suite of painted green furniture and a Japanese screen. Adjacent to it was the green Dressing Room containing some fine pieces of mahogany furniture.

The Servants Hall after restoration, prior to its dismantling for the Field Studies Centre.
(Arthur Rees, Port Talbot)

The Tower Room after restoration. Fitted window seats originally ran around the room.
(Arthur Rees, Port Talbot)

Another principal bedroom was the Yellow Bedroom, which contained a mahogany bedstead with fluted posts and green and gold curtains, matched by a suite of mahogany furniture. The Yellow Dressing Room lay next, containing another suite of mahogany furniture.

The South corridor on the first floor had six bedrooms, a bathroom and the nursery leading off it. All these rooms were furnished with a mixture of antique and Victorian pieces of furniture.

Five other bedrooms led off the north corridor on the first floor, whilst the corresponding corridors on the second floor had a similar number of bedrooms. On the third floor were smaller and more modestly furnished rooms for servants. In all, Margam Castle could boast 41 Bed and Dressing Rooms, of which some 25 were regarded as principal and guest bedrooms. When the mansion was originally built, it had only one bathroom, a common feature of most large country houses of the period where toilet facilities still tended to be rather spartan. By the early 20th century the house had a total of 8 bathrooms.

The Tower Room already mentioned, was a large room with specially fitted window seats arranged around the octagon, matched by a crimson carpet. It was a favourite summer retreat of the family.

There was to be no exception to Talbot's attention to detail and he devoted as much interest to the interior decoration and furnishings of his new house as he had to the design and exterior of the mansion. Letters plied back and forth to his agent, and in one dated 15th July 1840 from London, he writes: "The undermentioned dimensions I will thank you to get me accurately measured and sent me immediately. Size of the picture of Charles I and his family in the Library. Size of the three hunting pictures by Snyders in the Dining Room and the Tower. Size of the bases of all the vases. Number of yards in the rolls of Crimson Brussells carpet *last sent down* for the flooring of the great tower. Accurate measurements wanted." Later the same month, on the 21st, he tells Llewellyn: "I am in great need of the dimensions of the bases of the Busts at Margam and also the height and diameter of shaft base and capital of the yellow marble pillar in the library."

C. R, M, Talbot was an avid art collector and in this respect he certainly outshone his father, who had started the Talbot art collection following a 'Grand Tour' in the late 18th century, when he brought back a great deal of sculpture, antiquities and paintings from Italy. C. R. M. Talbot also travelled extensively abroad and purchased works of art which he sent back to Margam. He was also in regular attendance at Sale Rooms in this country, and Margam was soon filled with fine furniture, paintings and objects d'art. Talbot favoured artists of both the Dutch and Italian schools, although he purchased several works by French and British artists. He purchased important works attributed to Rubens, Rembrandt, Titian, Tiepelo, Teniers, Van Dyck, Salvator Rosa, Ruisdael, Frans Snyders, Aelbert Cuyp, Carraci, Berchem and Jan Both. Some of these acquisitions, formerly at Margam, have since found their way into public collections; these include 'The Story of Aristaeus' by Nicollo dell 'Abatte, 'Saint Cecilia' by Domenchino, and 'The Conversion of St. Paul' by Karel du jardin. These are now in the National Gallery in London. Another fine painting 'The Repose on the Flight to Egypt' by Gentileschi, was purchased in 1941 by the late Duke of Kent, from whose collection it passed into the Birmingham City Art Gallery. There were three alleged Canalettos at Margam, but two of these were added to the collection by Miss Emily C. Talbot later in the century.

Talbot's collection included several topographical pictures, together with some family portraits. Surprisingly he did not return the Mansel family portraits to Margam, but was content to leave them at Penrice. Possibly the sheer quantity of pictures he bought for Margam simply did not allow room for his ancestral portraits. He did however, return to Margam two superb topographical 'birdseye' views of the old Margam House in the late 17th century and these were proudly hung in the new house.

In addition to building the mansion house and lodges, C. R. M. Talbot was responsible for many new developments and improvements to the grounds and park at Margam. New carriage drives and approach roads were constructed, a variety of trees and shrubs were planted, and the grounds near the house and Orangery given special attention. No landscape architect was employed. Talbot merely had his own ideas carried out by the agents, gardeners and workforce. An account of 1832 gives us some idea of the work and cost involved in the new gardens':

July 4
Labourers employed preparing new garden £7 11s 8d
Jenkin Rees 1700 bricks 38 per t £32 6s 0d

Aug. 29
Hauling stone for garden wall £8 11s 8d

Nov. 21
William Kent Gardener & Persons preparing ground.
Taking down old walls Hauling Stone £13 8s 4d

One of the major garden schemes was the creation of a large Kitchen and Fruit garden by extending the existing park walls to include most of the old road and the village of Margam, necessitating the demolition of the Corner House Inn, two old barns and several cottages. Writing to Griffith Llewellyn in 1840, Talbot gives instructions regarding this new scheme:

". . . Regarding the garden, I send you a sketch on the other side. The gardener will please to take notice that he has no discretion whatever as to the situation or quantity of ground to be made use of. To the north of the wall no ground is to be appropriated to garden. It is my wish to build the wall, now, along the north side, but to place temporary fences to the east & west inclosures until I have finally settled the houses which may be removed from the village.

If necessary to drain the ground it should be done by means of a very deep drain outside, I think, because I am convinced that the land in that field is not naturally wet, but only soaky from the springs above, which might be cut off."

The sketch he refers to clearly shows the old road to Margam Abbey Church, proposed roads from the pound, the western approach to the new mansion and the proposed (and present) future road to the Church. Also shown are the location of two old barns which included portions of the old abbey. He also indicates his intention to demolish some houses the next year. In the event he allowed four of the old almshouses to remain. Margam village was finally swept away by 1842, by which time Talbot had built the picturesque new village of Groes.[6]

Although a very large greenhouse had been built at Margam in 1800, at the western end of the Orangery gardens, additional new greenhouses were now built near the north wall of the kitchen garden. In a few years, these kitchen gardens were to be producing vast quantities of fresh fruit and vegetables for the dining table, whilst surplus produce was allowed to be sold to estate tenants and employees. One later description of the Kitchen Gardens in 1885 is worth recounting:

"Arriving at one of the park entrances, we were met by our host of the day, Mr. Muir, head-gardener to Mr. Talbot. We were rather behind time, but not too late for a juicy cut from a leg of lamb and a savoury helping of rabbit pie, which was a credit to its maker. The vegetables had been put in the pot fresh from the garden, and I should have liked all my particular friends to have had an opportunity of giving their opinion as to the green peas, big as marbles, and sweet as peas should be. After the meal we took a stroll in the kitchen garden and gathered our dessert from the trees and bushes. Luscious peaches hung in rich profusion from the walls, cherries and gooseberries, strawberries and raspberries abounded everywhere. The garden is a large one, enclosed by tall walls, growing vegetables and fruits which frequently find their way into some of the larger shows of the county, and receive in substantial form the "well done" of the judges. The ground is well sheltered by the Big Wood, an immense tract of oak trees over eight hundred acres in extent."

The cultivation of indoor fruit also took place, with indoor peaches, nectarines and a variety of grapes grown in profusion, making the Vinery at Margam one of the best in Britain. A wide variety of flowers were cultivated including orchids and carnations. Trees and shrubs began to flourish in various parts of the ground, all carefully selected and positioned on Talbot's instructions.

Besides the gardens, Talbot had the small fishpond greatly enlarged in 1841 with a weir and head of water necessary for the supply of the ornamental fountains on the Orangery terrace. This terrace was constructed in 1852-53 with a low classical balustrade surmounted by urns and groups of cherubs, whilst two of the three fountains had stone dolphins supporting the fountain head.

The bridge near the fishpond was constructed in 1837 at the same time as the carriage drive, and Talbot was charged 7s 4d by one William Lewis & partners for "Making a new Bridge In the Great Park Leading to new house in Park." This latter bridge might possibly be a smaller bridge at the south west corner of the garden, below the west terrace and joining the gardens to the park over the ditch or ha-ha that extended along this stretch of ground. An interesting garden folly was created in the Orangery gardens to the west of the Orangery, by the careful dismantling in 1837 of the facade of the old Summer Banqueting House of the Mansel family, which had originally stood on the bank near the new house. This Banqueting House was reputedly designed by Inigo Jones, the famous 17th century architect. The facade was re-erected on its new site and formed the western end of a new cottage for the gardener, to be called Ivy Cottage. The niches of the facade were filled with 19th century statues representing the Four Seasons, which was to give the structure its local name of the Four Seasons Facade.

By the mid-19th century, Margam was a popular spot for visiting gentry to record in their topographical journals, just as it had been in the 18th century. Samuel Lewis in his Topographical Dictionary in 1840 writes: " ... A noble mansion, in the style of English architecture which prevailed in the reign of Henry VIII, has just been erected, on a scale suited to the rank and fortune of the representative of this ancient

Captain Andrew Talbot Fletcher (1880-1951).
(Author's Collection)

Emily Charlotte Talbot (1840-1918). Lithograph portrait c. 1900
(Author's Collection)

family." A few years later the genealogist William W. Mansel wrote in 1850: ".. . The Park, which is very extensive, well-wooded, and abundantly supplied with game, is still preserved in its original state. In the most desirable part of it, near the remains of the abbey, Mr. Talbot, the present M.P. for Glamorgan, has built a splendid Gothic residence. Its interior, while it embraces the convenience of a comfortable modern house, retains all the appearances of an ancient abbey, especially the staircase, which is in the centre of the house, and does infinite credit to the refined taste of the possessor, from whose plans the whole was raised. The exterior is richly ornamented with fretwork, and the emblem of the Mansells."

One frequent visitor to Margam during this period was Talbot's cousin, Henry Fox Talbot of Lacock. A pioneer photographer, he carried out several early experiments in the grounds of Margam Castle and succeeded in taking the earliest photographic views of the mansion which clearly shows the corner of the south west facade.

Later in the century, the Rev. F. 0. Morris in his 'Seats of Noblemen & Gentlemen of Great Britain & Ireland' (published c. 1880) enthuses that " . . . The house is a superb structure. The noble proportions of the principal rooms, the tapestried walls, the white marble floors, the beautiful pictures. give to Margam a magnificence in keeping with its beautiful surroundings. From the tower, which rises in the centre of the building, an extensive view of the surrounding countryside can be obtained. Behind rises a richly wooded hill, and in front is the Bristol Channel. The terraces around the Abbey present a charming appearance."

The gardens at Margam have an interesting link with royalty at this time, because the Prince and Princess of Wales (later Edward VII and Queen Alexandra) visited Margam on Monday, 17th October 1881. The royal couple stayed for luncheon after which the Princess planted a tree in the Orangery grounds.[7]

In 1886 the members of the Cambrian Archaeological Association visited Margam, touring the grounds and inspecting the Abbey Church, Ruins and Orangery. Their annual report records the visit thus: " . . . Here luncheon was served, and after thanks had been voted to Mr. Talbot for providing the party with wines on the occasion, and also for permission to inspect the ruins and the house, a move was made to the Chapter House, where Mr. Gamwell read a paper on the 'History of the Abbey' . . . Afterwards, the modern house, with its rich and handsome equipments, was inspected, as also were the fine paintings; two of the old house excited special interest."

Shortly after C. R. M. Talbot's death in 1890, his daughter and heiress., Miss Emily Charlotte Talbot (1840-1918) proceeded to make various alterations and improvements to the mansion and the grounds. Several rooms were redecorated, new bathrooms and plumbing installed, and various repairs and renovations made to the sixty year old building. The most important addition was that of a Billiards Room which was built over the site of the small inner courtyard, between the main apartments and domestic offices on the ground floor. Built in 1892, the Billiard Room was in the Jacobean style with light oak panelling around its walls, tall pilasters at each corner, with comfortable fixed seating on either side of a large billiard table. The room was lit by a large sky-light of plain and coloured glass with smaller round windows of coloured glass at each corner of the room. Elaborate Jacobean style plasterwork in a strap-work design decorated the arched recesses on each side of the room and around the fireplace. The fireplace itself had an elaborately carved wooden

The Castle in its heyday, showing the terrace, South and West Fronts. c.1900.

(Arthur Rees Collection)

South East View of the mansion, stables and Coach House. Photographed by Frederic Evans. c.1912.
(Author's Collection)

The West Lodge and approach to Margam Park. c.1920. This was demolished along with Groes Village in 1975.
(Barrie Flint Collection)

The East Lodges and Main Entrance Gates to Margam Park. c.1920.
(Barrie Flint Collection)

surround and overmantel bearing the date 1892 and the initials ECT for Emily Charlotte Talbot. The panelled walls were hung with antique weapons and armour. Since Miss Talbot frequently gave large house parties, the Billiard Room was a favourite retreat of the gentlemen guests at Margam in the late 19th and early 20th centuries. Miss Talbot also rehung many of the paintings, redecorated the library, had William Morris wallpaper hung in the Dining Room, and introduced a new and extensive central heating system to the principal rooms.

Miss Talbot also made several innovations in the grounds. A great many more trees and shrubs were planted, especially in the Orangery grounds where she preferred to see trees and shrubs with green foliage. Conifers and other trees and shrubs of a more sombre hue were considered by her more in keeping with the ruins and other buildings. Rhododendrons, azaleas, hydrangeas, magnolia, wisteria, myrtle and roses grew in profusion in various parts of the grounds. In the early 1900's, Miss Talbot had a Bamboo Garden created which contained many rare and beautiful plants. She also introduced a Pergola to the south western part of the Orangery garden; it was some 95 yards in length, formed of rustic oak and covered with roses of every possible colour and variety. At the same time, Miss Talbot had the south terrace of the Castle laid out with wide flower beds. Miss Talbot was in fact a most enthusiastic and knowledgeable gardener and was greatly helped by having for many years Robert Milner as her Head Gardener. Under Milner, the gardens at Margam Were to truly reach their zenith, and exhibits of fruit, flowers and vegetables from Margam regularly won prizes in County and National Horticultural Shows.

Following the death of Miss Talbot in 1918, her nephew, Captain Andrew Mansel Talbot Fletcher (1880-1951) inherited the Margam estate. Captain Fletcher owned and lived at an historic Scottish estate, Saltoun Hall in East Lothian, a large neo-Gothic mansion. He and his family frequently stayed at Margam, especially for the summer holidays. Although the Margam estate was administered by Trustees appointed under Miss Talbot's will, Captain Fletcher was able to implement some of his own ideas at Margam. He was responsible for the creation of New Pond in 1926 which he had constructed to improve the view from the house and at the same time give employment to the large number of local men without jobs. He also helped finance the famous plant explorer and botanist, Frank Kingdon-Ward (1885-1958), on one of his expeditions to the Himalayas. He brought back several plants and seeds for the park at Margam, including new varieties of Rhododendrons and Azaleas. The grounds at Margam were frequently opened to the public during Captain Fletcher's residence, and many fêtes and celebrations (including a Great Pageant in 1936) were held there.

Little alteration was carried out on the Castle during Captain Fletcher's ownership, other than essential repairs and decoration, with the notable exception of the Drawing Room which he had completely re-decorated at a cost of well over £2,000, shortly before the outbreak of the Second World War. He was also responsible for converting the old stable block into a Squash Court and Garage in 1930, and creating a tennis court to the south east of the mansion.

The Second World War saw the billeting of troops at Margam Castle, even while the Fletcher family were in residence. The Bachelor's wing, library and some outbuildings were requisitioned. Sadly, the Trustees of the Margam estate decided to sell the house and its contents, together with the major portion of the estate. Captain and Mrs. Fletcher were heartbroken at having to leave Margam and returned to Saltoun Hall. The famous auction house of Christies of London were given the task of

The West Front terrace. c.1925. The Library ran the length of this facade as far as the triple bay. The bay window on the right is the Drawing Room corner. On the first floor the Tapestry Bedroom was situated on the left, with the Chinese Bedroom, Dressing Rooms in central section, the Green Bedroom on the right.

(Author's Collection)

cataloguing the contents of the Talbot mansion, which were to be auctioned on the premises in a four-day sale between 27th and 30th October, 1941.

The Sale was to attract dealers and collectors from all over the country, as well as many local people anxious to have a last opportunity to view the treasures of Margam Castle and hopefully purchase an inexpensive memento. The first sale on the Monday was of the Silver plate and other objects of vertu, consisting of 152 lots. The silver was of mixed 18th and 19th century date, ranging from dinner services, dishes and vases to cutlery, candlesticks and candelabra. The highest price of the day was paid for an elegant dinner service, made up of mixed pieces dated 1788 and 1813, including pieces by the famous silversmith Paul Storr. The price realised was £500. Other items of interest included trophies and cups, and a collection of seventy-four Indian miniatures of potentates, palaces and mosques. A few silver presentation pieces were withdrawn from the sale and sent to the Fletchers at Saltoun. The first days' sale realised a total of £2,603 with very keen bidding.

The fine library of books was the next to be auctioned on the Tuesday, with well-known dealers like Quaritch, Maggs and Blackwell, together with representatives of public institutions like the Chief Librarian of the National Library of Wales. Over 300 lots were offered, consisting of books with coloured plates of the late 18th and early 19th centuries, runs of natural history journals, topographical volumes, and beautiful morocco bindings. Messrs. Quaritch paid the highest price of £205 for ten volumes of Sibthorp's 'Flora Graeca' (1806-40), whilst one of the library's treasures-the old English and Welsh Mss Chronicle on vellum of the 14th century, realised £145. The books raised even more than the silver, realising £3,189.

Wednesday saw the highlight of the four-day sale, with the disposal of the fine Talbot art collection of paintings and sculpture. This consisted of T. M. Talbot's collection of sculpture and ancient marbles, as well as C. R. M. Talbot's collection of paintings There were 464 lots in all, including some Talbot family portraits and two 17th century paintings of the old Mansel House, these last items being withdrawn from the sale and sent up to Saltoun. Connoisseurs, dealers and art experts from all over the country and a few from abroad, gathered for several hours brisk bidding. There was a dispute over the attribution of the Canalettos, particularly the one of Westminster. However, it succeeded in fetching a record £4,620. The National Gallery, represented by Sir Kenneth Clark, was able to secure the dell'Abbate of 'The Story of Aristaeus' for £300, whilst Gentileschi's 'Repose on the Flight to Egypt' was sold to the Duke of Kent for £399. Monamy's 'Shipping in a Calm' went for 440 guineas, as did a large painting 'The Concert of Birds' by Jan van Kessel. A beautiful Van Ruysdael landscape sold for 950 guineas, whilst the Rembrandt landscape was sold to a Dutch buyer at 2,300 guineas. The superb Veronese of the 'Madonna and Child in Glory' sold for 700 guineas. Seven Ibbetson watercolours of Welsh scenes were bought by the National Museum of Wales at a bargain 75 guineas. In comparison, the Greek vases and antique sculpture failed to reach large amounts, with only one lot-that of the head of a Roman boy-reaching over 100 guineas. A fine statue of a boy in Greek marble fetched only 50 guineas, and much of the sculpture was purchased by the second Lord Trent for his collection. Like most of the paintings, the sculpture was so widely dispersed it has been impossible to trace many items. However, two pieces are now in public collections; a bust of Pope Leo X by Christopher Hewetson is now in the Victoria and Albert Museum, whilst a figure of Diomedes by the Swedish sculptor, J. T. Sergel, is now in the National Museum in Stockholm. Sweden. One item was left unsold; this was a life-size statue in Thasian marble of an obscure Roman Emperor called Lucius Verus, which remained in the

Aerial View of the main house, stables and outbuildings. c.1958.
(Author's Collection)

Orangery and can still be seen today. The total raised by the sale of the sculptures and pictures was £16,365.

The last day saw the sale of the furniture, tapestries and household effects. These consisted of 995 lots including fine pieces of English, French and Italian furniture of 17th, 18th and 19th century date. Oak, mahogany, walnut, marquetry, ebony and boulle being in great evidence. Gilt chairs of the Louis XV and XVI period, Regency writing desks and tables, Georgian side tables, were mixed with Victorian mahogany or earlier English oak pieces. Great interest was shown in the sale of the contents of the Chinese Bedroom, where the ornate bedstead was sold for 29 guineas, whilst the beautiful hand painted wallpaper was sold with the proviso that it was to be removed at the purchaser's risk. It was actually sold for 28 guineas, but the purchaser does not appear to have made a great effort to remove the wallpaper, as it hung in tatters on surviving walls until as late as 1977. According to contemporary press reports, bidding was very keen and prices inflated due to wartime shortages and restrictions. One London dealer paid 125 guineas for an old English carpet, whilst six gilt fauteils fetched 100 guineas. Seven lots of old weapons and armour sold for £60 and a Persian carpet reached 65 guineas. A grand piano by Erard was sold for 25 guineas and a Regency harp by the same maker fetched only 51 guineas. The Georgian gilt side tables from the dining room, decorated in the manner of William Kent, sold for 65 guineas. A fine oak buffet carved with the Last Supper realised 32 guineas and a Louis XV marquetry commode was bought for 62 guineas. The four panels of Spanish petit-point needlework from above the main staircase were bought for 270 guineas, whilst the set of four beautiful Brussels tapestries from the Tapestry bedroom were sold to a London dealer for 600 guineas, the highest price of the day's sale. The last day of the sale had realised a total of £4,314.

The four-day sale had realised £29,213 and the contents of Margam Castle were soon dispersed leaving an empty and forlorn mansion. The castle continued in the occupation of troops during the war, both British and American. In 1942 the estate was purchased by David M. Evans-Bevan of Cadoxton, Neath. Evans-Bevan was a well-known local businessman whose family owned local collieries and the Vale of Neath Brewery. Shortly after purchasing the estate, he took up residence at the former agent's house of Twyn-yr-hydd. There has been much local speculation as to the damage done to the castle at this time by the troops, but little real damage was done, as admitted by Evans-Bevan who stated that: "There was some damage done, but nothing in excess of what is normally done in an occupation of this nature." The real damage was caused after the troops had left, with the vandalism and continued neglect of the empty house.

At the end of the war and following its de-requisitioning, the castle remained empty. Sir David Evans-Bevan felt it was too large and uncomfortable a house to live in, choosing instead to continue to live in Twyn-yr-hydd. In 1942 he generously offered the castle as a gift to St. Michael's Theological College, Llandaff for institutional use. Unfortunately the college declined it owing to the great expense needed for necessary adaptations. In 1955 the Association of Conservative Clubs intimated to Evans-Bevan that they might be interested in using the castle as a convalescent home. However, by this time the state of the castle was rather serious and considerable expense would have been needed for urgent renovations, even before any conversion to an institutional use. Therefore the idea was reluctantly abandoned.

West Glamorgan Firemen fighting the blaze at the North Front. 4th August, 1977.
(Peter Knowles, Port Talbot)

A leading article in the 'Port Talbot Guardian' for July 19, 1957 carried the heading 'Margam Castle is Going to Ruin'. The article lamented the decay of the mansion and reported that "The interior of the building is in a very bad state of disrepair. Walls have collapsed and ceilings and floors have all decayed away." The article went on to say "The last hope of saving Margam Castle is gone ... now it will be left to a long and lingering death. Over the years, various plans were suggested for using the mansion, ranging from a Country Club to a residential Conference Centre for the Steel Company. Even Sir David himself seems to have second thoughts about making use of the castle and had plans drawn up in 1963 to convert the mansion into more practical residential accommodation. However, all these ideas were to come to nothing.

Refusing to instal a caretaker in the building, Evans-Bevan left the mansion a prey to vandals, thieves and decay. The lead on the roof and from the pipes was stolen, vandals attacked the interior; and broken windows and leaking roofs allowed rainwater to seep into the once stately rooms. Plasterwork crumbled, carved woodwork and panelling rotted away, wall-coverings became sodden and hung in rotting tatters on the walls. Only the stables and outbuildings were maintained and continued in use The interior was slowly gutted for some of its more useful fixtures. Huge timbers were removed from between the ground floor library and the bedrooms above, removed on the orders of the owner to furnish 'antique' beams for a Vale of Neath Brewery hostelry !

On rare and infrequent occasions, the grounds were thrown open to the public. Ironically, Margam played host to one Open Day to mark European Conservation Year on August 22nd, 1970, its overgrown grounds and terraces, crumbling Orangery and Castle, a topic of conversation for the visitors.

Fortunately, the year 1973 saw Sir David Evans-Bevan preparing to sell the Margam estate. Admirable judgement and foresight by the Glamorgan County Council, led and encouraged by Lord Heycock, saw the eventual purchase of the historic and beautiful estate for the sum of £400,000. Even with the sale of the estate, the mansion was not to be spared further insults Although the castle was a statutory listed or protected building, Evans-Bevan removed some remaining fixtures, including the marble fireplaces of the library and drawing-room, which were to be re-erected in his new home in Jersey. Margam Castle was already a gutted and derelict shell when the County Council purchased the estate.

The programme of restoration and improvement by the County Council was continued by the new authority of West Glamorgan from 1974. Unfortunately, the vast amount of work to be done and the urgent need to save the beautiful Georgian Orangery, necessarily meant that the Castle had to be virtually last on the list of priorities However, some clearance work was undertaken in the removal of debris from the interior of the main house and outbuildings. The stables and former Squash Court were renovated and an Interpretative Centre with an exhibition of Margam's history opened in June 1977. More recent work includes the opening of an Audio-Visual Theatre, the 'Coach House Theatre' in July 1981.The renovation work here was carried out by a team of youngsters employed under the Manpower Services Commission, who have undertaken a programme of similar work at the park in the past few years.

At approximately 10 a.m. on the morning of Thursday, August 4th, 1977, fire broke out in the roof of Margam Castle. Workmen clearing debris and rotten timbers, had begun to burn timbers in an open fireplace, with the result that the chimney and then the roof caught fire. The fire quickly spread, taking hold of exposed and rotten timbers, within minutes the west wing was ablaze. West Glamorgan firemen summoned to the scene fought to stop the blaze spreading, but unfortunately the decayed state of the building and a southwesterly wind drove the fire into the south wing and the centre of the castle. Flames leaped and danced through broken windows and above the battlements. Crashing timbers and masonry, splintering glass and the crackle of flames, together with the acrid smoke, completed the devastating scene. For a long time the great octagonal tower was obscured by clouds of billowing smoke from the blazing building. Firemen pumped water from the nearby fishpond, and fought strenuously to prevent the fire reaching the entrance hall and north wing of the castle. The fierce blaze took over five hours to bring under control, by which time the entire west and south wings, together with the Billiard Room and southern domestic offices were a gutted shell. Firemen remained to keep a watch overnight.

Within a few days, the County Engineer's Department had carried out an inspection to ascertain the condition of the structure. It was eventually decided to continue with the clearance work and stabilise the building before attempting any further work. This was successfully done between 1977 and 1979 with the aid of the job Creation Scheme under the supervision of the County Planning, Architects and Engineer's Departments. One interesting find during clearance work at this time, was the discovery of a 19th century mason's mallet behind the plaster in a wall of the staircase hall. In addition, two fine bronze cannon bearing the Mansel crest were discovered in the old plate safe.

The future of the Castle is certainly hopeful and local people were encouraged by the new scheme whereby redundant trainee carpenters, bricklayers, plasterers and plumbers were involved in a scheme run by the Construction Industry Training Board with the co-operation of the West Glamorgan County Council. Early in 1981 these young apprentices started to carry out renovations to the North wing of the mansion, and will eventually restore this wing, together with the Entrance Hall and several outbuildings around the courtyards. During the next two years, work is also expected to be carried out on the Staircase Hall and Tower.

The marble floor of the Entrance Hall showing the Maunch motif.
(D. John Adams, Port Talbot)

RESTORATION & RENEWAL 1982 - 1998

Despite increasing budget and financial strictures during the last decade or so of its existence, West Glamorgan County Council continued its brave programme of renovation and restoration. The North Wing was reroofed in 1982, using many of the original slates, the work being undertaken by the established local firm of David & Harold Wilson. Work also continued on the stabilising and consolidation of the walls, chimneys and turrets of the south and west wings. The stonework of the central gable above the west bays had collapsed during the 1977 fire, and this was rebuilt to incorporate a new stone shield depicting the West Glamorgan County Council Coat of Arms. Internal renovation was to be concentrated on the North Wing and Entrance Hall, with approval given in 1984 for an £86,000 restoration scheme as the first stage in the rescue plan. Electricity was reintroduced to the mansion for the second time in its history, since it was originally installed in 1891 as part of Miss Talbot's modernisation of the house between 1890 and 1893. The park staff moved into offices located in the renovated first floor of the North Wing in 1985, whilst the ground floor was later opened as an exhibition and interpretative area replacing the original exhibition space removed for the expansion of the park shop. The original servants hall was refurbished and furnished with antique furniture loaned by the Welsh Folk Museum.

The County Council launched a search for private investors to carry out further restoration and development, with suggestions that the castle could be converted into a hotel. Complete restoration was estimated at £3 million, and although grants would be available the Council was not in a position to fund such an expensive scheme. In 1987 the most ambitious part of the restoration programme was under way with the reinstatement of the elaborate plasterwork and fan-vaulting of the entrance hall, and the great staircase ceiling beneath the tower, expertly restored by master craftsmen. At the same time the Tower Room with its superb views over the park and surrounding countryside was also restored.The complete restoration of the Tower was carried out by the firm of Ernest Ireland of Bath, whilst the new plasterwork of the Entrance Hall was crafted by Terry and Keith Moyle.

In November, 1987 a rare daguerreotype of the Castle from the south east, taken by C.R.M.Talbot's great friend, the Reverend Calvert Jones of Swansea, was put up for sale by Talbot's descendants. It sold at Christies for a record sum of £14,300 to an American gallery. This unique picture, probably the earliest view of the castle and one of the first photographs taken in Wales, was fortunately saved by the government refusal of an export licence, and ultimately purchased by the National Library of Wales. The daguerreotype was later exhibited at Margam Orangery for a brief period in April 1991.

Proposals to turn the Castle into a luxury hotel were given a further boost in 1989 when the developers Grand Metropolitan and other leading financial institutions took an interest, although the plan did not materialise. The completion of the restoration of the entrance hall, particularly the reinstatement of the spectacular fan-vaulted ceiling with its plaster pendants, saw the official opening on the 14th April 1992 by the Chairman of the County Council, Councillor Brian Ludlam. The original gothic style panelling had been badly damaged and only a small section could be saved, but from this plaster copies had been made and painted to resemble wood. Whilst the two large windows were reglazed, it was not possible to reinstate the badly damaged and remaining stained glass. Modern coloured glass insets depicting the

Mansel and Talbot coat of arms, were designed by the Swansea College of Art Stained Glass Department, and placed at the apex of the Gothic arched window over the main doors. A generous donation was made by Lady Eira Evans Bevan, together with donations from British Oxygen, Port Talbot Historical Society, and Timothy Hancorn of Port Talbot, towards the restoration of the heraldic stained glass. Unfortunately, to date this glass has not been completely restored or returned to Margam, although funds and plans are in hand. It had not been possible to restore the badly damaged and impressive marble floor of the entrance hall, although a most generous offer to pay for its restoration was made in 1989 by J.T.Talbot Fletcher, the last heir to Margam. Sadly this offer had not been taken up by the time of his death in 1995. A small historical exhibition was opened in the partly restored staircase hall, and the general public allowed access to this part of the castle for the first time in many years. Work also continued on the renovation of the castle outbuildings and courtyards.

The staircase hall was the impressive venue for a Musica Rediviva, the first musical recital to take place in the mansion since before the 2nd World War. On a fine summers evening on 24th July, 1992, guests were entertained to a memorable musical evening by the Cwmavon born international mezzo-soprano Anna Risi, accompanied by the Ukrainian composer and instrumentalist Alla Sirenko. This cultural landmark was to be followed by another Musica Rediviva in July 1993 by Miss Risi and the Velca Ladies Choir from Rome.

The year 1995 saw the final phase of a £300,000 restoration project with the re-roofing of the mansion's South and West Wings. In April, huge roof trusses were lifted into place by crane, and slate from North Wales was used for the vast expanse of roof. The cost of restoring the North Wing and Tower had been £150,000. The sale of cottages in the park, together with substantial grants from CADW (Welsh Historic Monuments), and the Welsh Church Acts Fund, enabling completion of the first major phase of restoration. Unfortunately, by now the cost of a full restoration was estimated at a staggering £6.5 million. The County Council continued to explore and consider various ways of using the Castle to best advantage. Converting part of the interior for use as a restaurant, banqueting hall, tea-rooms, local and natural history exhibition rooms, gallery, craft centre, private apartments, and a Welsh Photography Museum, were all suggested. Fortunately, funds were made available for the replacement of the numerous sash windows, and during this part of the restorations, several masons marks were discovered including that of Mathew Alderson, who worked on the castle until 1841. Another craftsman, James Parry, recorded his name for posterity by indicating that the window frames were made in Shrewsbury in 1831 and hanging the sashes in the winter of 1833.

By the end of 1995 craftsmen had started to replace the long lost floorboards of the upper floors. An official ceremony to mark the completion of the restoration work to date, was held on the 1st March 1996, when the Bishop of Llandaff, the Right Reverend Roy Davies, unveiled a commemorative plaque on the half-landing of the main staircase. Various plans and proposals continued to be considered for the future use of the Castle. In addition to those mentioned earlier, use as a hotel or health farm as part of a multi-million pound leisure development of the park, with plans for a theme park at the eastern end of the park, were also put forward. Following local government re-organisation in April 1996, the West Glamorgan County Council ceased to exist and Margam Park became the responsibility of the newly created County Borough of Neath Port Talbot which has continued the restoration programme.

In late August 1997, the castle opened its doors to visitors and played host to the South Wales Model, Craft and Hobby Show. Architectural salvage was moved from the Library and Drawing Room to allow model displays and public access. For the first time in nearly fifty years it was possible to walk through the now skeletal rooms on both the ground and first floors. The campaign to find a suitable home for the proposed Welsh Assembly in 1997-98 provided the County Borough Council with the impetus to make a further suggestion for the utilization of Margam Castle. The idea gained support locally, but was eventually rejected.

At the same time, plans were revealed which gave further hope for the Castle's future. A multi-million pound redevelopment scheme is centred on a unique residential field studies centre, jointly funded by the County Borough Council and the Field Studies Council. The North Wing will house dormitories and bedrooms, together with classrooms and laboratories, for use by school parties and adult courses from Wales and further afield. The latest computer equipment will be installed providing a vivid contrast to the ancient walls of the former grandiose Talbot mansion. Ultimately, it is hoped to utilize the south and west wings for the centre, as well as providing public exhibition areas. Inevitably, the new plans for Margam will bring changes. The current exhibitions in the Servant's Hall and Housekeeper's Room will be dismantled, as will the Coach House theatre. The latter is being turned into a new pond life centre which will include natural history exhibits and an ambitious indoor cascade or waterfall. The park offices will be relocated in the old laundry, more recently used as a Field Studies classroom. It is interesting to note that to date over £500,000 has been spent on the Castle's renovations, with two-thirds of the main house still in need of restoration and refurbishment. This is ten times the cost of building the Castle in the early nineteenth century, when Christopher Talbot's well spent £50,000 was considered extravagant.

NOTES

1. C.R.M.Talbot was called 'Kit' by his family and friends.

2. Now the Park Shop.

3. The stained glass from the East Window was removed in 1978 by the Stained Glass Department of Swansea College of Art, for conservation work prior to its re-setting.

4. Some of the stalls were salvaged and installed in the foyer of the Coach House Theatre, and later removed to the Staircase Hall.

5. Now in the Margam Road Presbyterian Church, Port Talbot.

6. The picturesque village of Groes was demolished in 1975 to make way for the new M4 motorway extension.

7. It is perhaps interesting to note a more modern link between the Margam Gardens and another Prince and Princess of Wales, as a spray of Orange blossom from Margam was affixed to the carriage of the bride and bridegroom for the wedding of H.R.H. the Prince of Wales and Lady Diana Spencer on the 29th July, 1981.

BIBLIOGRAPHY AND SOURCES

ADAMS, D. John: Glimpses of Margam Life 1830-1918 (1986)

ADAMS, D. John & REES, Arthur: A Celebration of Margam Park and Gardens (1989)

AP GWILYM: The Red Dragon, Vol. VIII, 1885

ARCHAEOLOGIA CAMBRENSIS, 1886

COLVIN, Howard: A Biographical Dictionary of British Architects (1978)

DOWSLAND, Frank L.: Thomas Hopper, 1776-1851 Architect (Thesis for Dip. Arch., University of Durham, 1962)

FRANKLIN, Jill: The English Gentleman's Country House and its Plan 1835-1914 (1981)

GlROUARD, Mark: The Victorian Country House (1979)

HANSON, J. Ivor: Profile of a Welsh Town (1968)

HOBBS, John L.: The Haycocks Changed the Face of Shrewsbury (article in the Shropshire Magazine, February 1960)

JONES, Anthony: Heraldry in Glamorgan. Mid & West Glamorgan No.1. The Abbey Church of St. Mary, Margam, and Margam Castle (1993)

LEWIS, Samuel: Topographical Dictionary of Wales (1840)

MACAULEY, James: The Gothic Revival (1975)

MARGAM CASTLE Christies Sales Catalogues, 27-30 October, 1941

MARGAM CASTLE Sale Catalogue, 1942

MORRIS, Rev. F.O.: Picturesque Views of Seats of Noblemen & Gentlemen of Great Britain & Ireland (c.1880)

SEARLE, Arthur: Thomas Hopper (article in The Essex Journal, 1970)

THOMAS, Hilary M.: Margam Estate Management 1765-1860 (article in The Glamorgan Historian, Vol. VI, 1969)

TRANSACTIONS of the Aberafan & Margam Historical Society, Vol. VI, 1933-34.

TRANSACTIONS of the Port Talbot Historical Society, Vol. II, No.1, 1969.

Manuscript Sources include the Penrice & Margam MSS in the National Library of Wales; the Traherne-Mansel Franklen MSS in the National Library of Wales; the Margam Estate Records in the West Glamorgan Record Office; the Lacock Abbey MSS; personal correspondence 1968-1980, together with various local newspaper accounts of the 1941 Sale.